HOW SHOULD PRISONS TREAT INMATES?

Other Books in the At Issue Series:

Affirmative Action
Animal Experimentation
Anorexia
Anti-Semitism
Biological and Chemical Weapons
Child Labor and Sweatshops
Child Sexual Abuse
Cloning
Date Rape
Does Capital Punishment Deter Crime?
Drugs and Sports
The Ethics of Abortion
The Ethics of Euthanasia
The Ethics of Human Cloning
Ethnic Conflict
Food Safety
The Future of the Internet
Gay Marriage
Guns and Crime
Heroin
Immigration Policy
Interracial Relationships
Legalizing Drugs
Marijuana
The Media and Politics
Nuclear and Toxic Waste
Nuclear Security
Physician-Assisted Suicide
Rainforests
Rape on Campus
Sex Education
Sexually Transmitted Diseases
Single-Parent Families
Smoking
The Spread of AIDS
Teen Suicide
UFOs
The United Nations
U.S. Policy Toward China
Violent Children
Voting Behavior
Welfare Reform

HOW SHOULD PRISONS TREAT INMATES?

Michele Wagner, *Book Editor*

David L. Bender, *Publisher*
Bruno Leone, *Executive Editor*
Bonnie Szumski, *Editorial Director*
Stuart B. Miller, *Managing Editor*

An Opposing Viewpoints® Series

Greenhaven Press, Inc.
San Diego, California

Library of Congress Cataloging-in-Publication Data

How should prisons treat inmates? / Michele Wagner, book editor.
        p.   cm. — (At issue)
    Includes bibliographical references and index.
    ISBN 0-7377-0547-7 (pbk. : alk. paper). — ISBN 0-7377-0548-5
    (lib. bdg. : alk. paper)
    1. Prisoners—United States. 2. Imprisonment—United States.
I. Wagner, Michele, 1975– II. Series: At issue (San Diego, Calif.)

HV9471 .H68 2001
365'.6'0973—dc21   00-037560

© 2001 by Greenhaven Press, Inc., PO Box 289009,
San Diego, CA 92198-9009

Printed in the U.S.A.

Table of Contents

		Page
Introduction		6
1.	Prison Should Be Uncomfortable *Joe Arpaio with Len Sherman*	8
2.	Violent Offenders Should Be Placed in Supermax Prisons *California Department of Corrections*	16
3.	Strict Discipline Lowers Prison Violence *Christopher Drew*	20
4.	Working Prisoners Benefit the Economy *Morgan O. Reynolds*	27
5.	Jail: Rough Road or Easy Street? *Dana Tofig*	34
6.	Convicted Felons Deserve the Right to Vote *Jamie Fellner and Marc Mauer*	40
7.	Supermax Prisons Are Cruel and Inhumane *Spencer P.M. Harrington*	51
8.	Electronic Weapons Should Not Be Used to Control Prisoners *William F. Schulz*	62
9.	Prisoners Should Receive Humane End-of-Life Care *Nancy Neveloff Dubler*	71
10.	Chain Gangs Should Be Abolished *Tracy L. Meares*	85
11.	Sexual Abuse of Women Inmates Is Widespread *Nina Siegal*	89
Organizations to Contact		98
Bibliography		102
Index		104

Introduction

Imprisonment as punishment for crimes was first used during the sixteenth century in Europe. Prior to that, criminal correction usually consisted of enslavement or swift physical punishment such as whipping or execution. Prison was conceived as a more humane response to criminal behavior. When Europeans established colonies in America in the seventeenth century they continued the practice of imprisoning those convicted of crimes.

During the colonial era, the number of Americans in prison made up a small, barely noticeable segment of the population. That situation has changed dramatically, however. According to statistics from the Department of Justice's Bureau of Justice, if incarceration rates continue unchanged, 1 out of every 20 Americans alive today will be imprisoned at some time in their lives.

This rate of incarceration has increased quite recently. In 1980, 139 of every 100,000 Americans were incarcerated; in 1996, that number had nearly quadrupled to 427 per 100,000, according to Bureau of Justice statistics. This is due in part to new crime laws such as "three strikes and you're out" and tougher sentencing for drug-related offenses.

More focus on punishment

The "get tough on crime" stance that many politicians have adopted is finding its way into America's corrections system as the prison population continues to grow. The people are tired of crime, and some politicians note this and respond by advocating harsher treatment of convicted criminals. Some political leaders contend that inmates forfeit most or all of their rights the moment they enter prison and therefore are subject to measures designed to punish rather than rehabilitate. As Michigan state senator Phil Hoffman (R.) says, "We're a baby-sitting service for adults who have raped us, robbed us and murdered us."

In an atmosphere in which the focus is increasingly on punishment, legislators and the public are becoming fed up with prisoners living in what some characterize as resort-like facilities with privileges such as cable TV, weightlifting rooms, free education, and libraries. Many Americans would like to reduce or eliminate such prison amenities to cut down on prison spending and redirect that money toward fighting and preventing crime.

In addition to generally reducing inmates' privileges, many states have also developed "super-max" prisons, designed to house the most troublesome prisoners. In these facilities, prisoners spend 23 hours a day locked alone in their cells. They are allowed no contact with other prisoners and minimal contact with guards. They are offered no educational or vocational training and usually no television or reading material. Supporters of "super-max" prisons say they are necessary tools to punish otherwise incorrigible prisoners. In that same vein, officials in many prisons where violence is prevalent have acquired shock devices for control of violent or uncooperative prisoners.

Another popular idea among tough-on-crime policymakers has been putting able-bodied prisoners to work for private contractors. The money earned by the correctional institutions under such arrangements can be used to offset prison costs. A fringe benefit is that prisoners also learn skills they can use after being released. But not every prison-work program imparts such skills to inmates. In some states, chain gangs have been reinstated to provide a source of laborers, as well as to drive home the point that prison life is not pleasant.

Concerns about abuses

However, there is another side to the treatment of inmates. Supporters of prisoners' rights contend that harsher punishment and stricter discipline has led to a system rife with human rights violations. In 1998, for example, Amnesty International released a report on prison conditions in the United States titled *Rights for All*. The report cites numerous examples of human rights violations ranging from physical to sexual to psychological abuse of prisoners. Sexual abuse of the growing number of women inmates is a major focus of pro-prisoner groups. Amnesty International's research indicates that nearly every woman incarcerated today has been sexually abused in some way during her imprisonment.

Those who are critical of get-tough-on-prisoners measures are also concerned about the use of shock devices for the control of prisoners. Critics contend that the potential for abuse is too great with a device that can deliver a 50,000-volt shock from 300 feet away, as stun belts can. Some observers note that studies have not yet ruled out the possibility of long-term damage on prisoners corrected with these devices.

In addition to being concerned about physical abuse, advocates of inmates' rights believe that privileges for prisoners are important. These individuals argue that prisoners who are denied recreation, learning, or hot meals will only become angrier, more violent, and more likely to commit another crime after their release. Prisoners' rights advocates also decry "super-max" prisons for the same reasons, believing that the treatment prisoners receive in these facilities only makes them more savage and less inclined towards rehabilitation.

Health care in prisons is also a concern for inmates' rights advocates, who contend that changes need to be made in most prison health care systems to accommodate the needs of elderly or terminally ill prisoners. The current priorities of security and cost control, some contend, should not prevent inmates from receiving care comparable to what is available to members of the community outside the prison's walls.

The differing opinions on how prisons should treat their inmates parallels society's deeper concern of how to control and eliminate crime. The contributors to *At Issue: How Should Prisons Treat Inmates?* consider whether "supermax" prisons are humane and effective; what kinds of amenities and privileges prisoners should have, if any; whether or not shock devices are an acceptable means of discipline; the end-of-life care that prisoners receive; sexual abuse of women prisoners; the legitimacy of chain gangs; and the benefits of prison labor. The authors confront these issues in an attempt to dissect and understand the numerous legal, ethical and moral concerns involved in how prisons treat inmates.

1

Prison Should Be Uncomfortable

Joe Arpaio with Len Sherman

Joe Arpaio is the elected sheriff of Maricopa County, Arizona. Prior to that he was a federal drug enforcement agent for almost thirty years, working undercover in Turkey, South America, and other locations.

Jail should be uncomfortable, though not unsafe. Under Sheriff Arpaio's jail program in Maricopa County, Arizona, inmates do not have access to frills such as coffee, cigarettes, and most television. Some prisoners live in tent cities in the Arizona desert, which reduces costs for housing, and almost all prisoners work. These measures are needed to make jail an adequate form of punishment.

While the tents [housing for inmates] are the most substantial and visible part of our jail program, they do not stand alone. Other measures also embody my philosophy of making the entire Maricopa County jail system less pleasant, more efficient and less burdensome on the taxpayers.

The bottom line can be summed up in a line I constantly repeat: *Our inmates should never live better in jail than they do on the outside.* It's that simple. Jail should be a place nobody ever wants to return to. That doesn't mean that inmates should be treated cruelly or inhumanely. Such behavior is not only ethically and legally unacceptable, it also is not productive from an institutional viewpoint. Indeed, arbitrary or barbaric management merely serves to render any jail more violent, unruly, and dangerous for both inmates and guards. Jail should be uncomfortable, not unsafe. Thus, the key concepts underlying my *modus operandi* are discipline, hard work, and a total absence of frills.

Once again, keep in mind that these measures apply to all Maricopa County jails, tent and hard facility, canvas and concrete.

Eliminating frills, keeping the basics

We start with the prohibitions I instituted: No smoking. No *Playboys, Penthouses*, or any nude magazines. No coffee. No violent television shows. No "NC- 17," "R," or "PG" movies.

(I cut out movies altogether after I showed *Old Yeller* and the inmates wildly cheered when the poor dog died.)

The prisoners don't like it. Every time I visit the tents, I hear the same thing: Why can't we have coffee? Why can't we have cigarettes? And my answer is always the same: Because you're in jail! (The irony, of course, is that by helping them quit smoking or, to a lesser extent, stop consuming coffee, we're actively promoting their health and well-being, whether they want to or not, whether they like it or not.)

It may be hard to believe, but many inmates cannot seem to grasp that some of the rights and privileges they enjoy on the outside are forfeited the moment they are incarcerated. For too many inmates, jail is simply a way station, even a respite, between other criminal destinations. One day they might be scoring in a crack house, another day breaking into someone's home, another in custody, another back on the streets, on and on, round and round they go, smoothly moving from one stop in their desultory life journey to another. You might be surprised to discover how basic are the needs of many criminals: Food, shelter, television, cigarettes, drugs, sex. As long as they can satisfy those desires, they are momentarily content. So when they move from the street, where they might have been mugging or robbing or dealing or even murdering to get what they want, to the penitentiary, and find that they can live just about as well or even better, without having to put out any effort (even criminal effort), what do you think is the result? What do you think *they* think? Do you think they fear jail? Do you think they pause before hitting a little old lady over the head to steal her bag and say to themselves, "Gee, maybe I shouldn't do this because if I'm caught I'll have to go back to that terrible place? That place where I can't smoke, have coffee, eat steak, do drugs, and have sex."

Of course not.

Many inmates cannot seem to grasp that some of the rights and privileges they enjoy on the outside are forfeited the moment they are incarcerated.

Instead, they say, "Hey, being locked up wasn't so bad. I did pretty much anything I wanted, I had my conjugal visits, and my friends brought me drugs, and I could buy cigarettes in the commissary, and the food was better than I was used to, and I got to sit around all day watching TV and lifting weights." Even if they are caught and convicted, they know they have a good chance of getting a deal from the overworked assistant district attorney, and getting probation from the overloaded court. And even if they are sent away, they know they probably won't get too much time, and even if they do, they know they'll probably serve only one-third of their sentence, getting out for "good behavior," whatever that fraudulent term means, or even get kicked loose, free and clean, only because the warden's jails are busting at the seams, and the warden decides the easiest way to deal with the problem is to just open the doors and let out a bunch of convicts.

So what's there to worry about? What's there to fear? You know the old saying, "Don't do the crime if you can't do the time"? That used to mean something, something to consider long and hard. Now it's a joke. "Do the time?" Fat chance!

So I'm doing what I can to alter the penal equation. I'm not in charge of the courts or the county attorney's office. I am in charge of my deputies and my jails, and I have been changing the way my institutions handle their responsibilities.

Other than the tents, the most attention I've received from the public and the press concerns the green bologna. That green bologna, comprised of part fact, part fiction, is only the most famous piece of the entire food story, a story with which you should be more familiar.

And don't fret; I'll explain about the green bologna in short order.

The Board of Supervisors slashed my department's budget soon after I took office. My ongoing efforts to uncover ways of tightening up control of the jails, toughening up the system, and sparing taxpayer funds, now took on extra urgency.

The not-so-secret secret to increasing efficiency is thinking creatively; contemplating angles others haven't contemplated, mediating on solutions untried and untested. That's precisely what we did with our food service.

Thinking creatively

Before I was elected, the Maricopa County Sheriff's Office (MCSO) food service operated pretty similarly to every other sheriff department's food service. The service purchased food based strictly on the low bidder system—the manufacturer or supplier whose prices were the lowest for a particular item won our business. That's certainly a fair and straightforward system, but not necessarily the best. In other words, working solely through low bids does not necessarily maximize the assets available both in and out of our department.

So we changed the way we did business. In the process, we tried some things nobody had done before. We mixed it up, combining some old ideas with some new ones, and discovered a slew of options that fulfilled a variety of requirements.

Frank Russo, our food service manager, came up with one terrific innovation. One way to preserve food, and thus save money by not having to throw out whatever is not immediately used, is—stated as simply as possible—to cook food at 165 degrees, bag it in cryovac bags, and then place the bags in refrigerators or freezers set at a temperature of 40 degrees or lower. In short, this is a method of pasteurization.

So far, so good. The rub begins when we consider that the apparatus used to accomplish this is called the Cook Chill System, and costs in the neighborhood of half a million dollars. That's half a million my department absolutely did not have.

So Frank improvised. He gathered together four hundred steam kettles, each kettle capable of holding one hundred gallons, and called a company that modified the kettles. The company attached pumps and whatnot, and suddenly we were the proud owners of an almost homemade Cook Chill System, capable of preparing and preserving everything from beef stew to vegetables to spaghetti sauce, all for the bargain basement price of $80,000.

Another innovation: Many local farmers have responded to our money-saving efforts by donating parts of other fields for our use. Thus, we have five department trucks that take inmates out to pick these fields for whatever is waiting for us, be it tomatoes or potatoes, carrots or cauliflower. The farmers are then given receipts so they can write off what is taken as tax-deductible contributions.

At this point, we are receiving so many contributions from farmers that our five trucks are not sufficient, and we are renting several more to meet the demand.

All this effort has paid a most important side benefit. In late 1993, George Graves of Distribution and Food Services was assigned to find "free" food. As I have just described, George was wildly successful. But his labors did not end there.

In the course of making contacts with farmers, George became aware of the Arizona Gleaning Coalition, a consortium of growers, private corporations, state agencies, and food banks.

At first, MCSO was only a recipient of surplus food from this network. Quickly, however, George realized that MCSO had resources that the coalition needed. He realized that MCSO could enter into a very fruitful partnership with the coalition, and that something very exciting could emerge from this union. And so we started to use our trucks to transport food around the state, picking up from farmers and other providers and bringing it to food banks. The impact of this intensified distribution is clear: Since March 1994, the Arizona Gleaning Coalition estimates that food distribution has doubled to food banks throughout the state, food that otherwise would have gone to waste. We're talking about more than $800,000 in food product.

In addition, George has arranged for the assignment of working inmates to all of the valley food banks, providing the charities with a reliable labor supply.

George Graves has been named to the Coalition's Operations Committee, and continues to work to further its laudable goals, both at the office and at home. For his inspiring example, George received a special commendation from the Sheriffs Office in 1995.

The truth is, I don't think these measures are that tough, they're just common sense.

Our relationship to the farming community continues to grow, sometimes in unexpected directions. For example, we have been giving our garbage to pig farmers, garbage being a pig delicacy. In return, every now and then the pig farmers supply us with a couple of animals, which we have slaughtered and then cooked.

Then there's our computer system. Actually, it's just a pair of PCs backed up by a fax machine. The fax is tied into a network of food vendors and manufacturers, and we are constantly searching for special buys. For example, we might call Oscar Meyer and find out whether they have any products that could be labeled "seconds" for sale. Seconds are not spoiled or distressed products, but foodstuffs that have some cosmetic defect that renders them unsuitable for the retail market. It's no different than going to a clothing outlet store and paying just a few dollars for an expensive garment that is marked down, because a few stitches are out of line, or a button is missing. That's what we do every day, seeking out those discounts and deals.

And Oscar Meyer is very happy to respond, because the company is glad to help out law enforcement and also because the company is glad to have a market for what is none-too-marketable. Oscar Meyer has sold us sliced turkey, salami, olive loaf, pimento loaf, and, yes, bologna. We'll take whatever the company has to offer, and we've paid as little as twenty-eight cents per pound. Along with Oscar Meyer, we deal with a host of other major concerns, including Kellogg's, Armour, and Swift.

And don't neglect the savings from even an isolated measure like cutting out coffee, because cutting out coffee saved $100,000 a year. In similar fashion, the switch to cold meals saved another $400,000.

Our system works so well that we get calls from prison and jail systems from Maine to New York to California asking for advice and assistance.

We've received so much media attention for our efforts to hold down costs that some vendors have contacted us with substantial donations. For instance, not long ago a New York manufacturer heard about what we were doing out here in Maricopa County, and contributed 450 cases of corn dogs, each case containing a hefty seventy-two corn dogs. The manufacturer donated the dogs for less than the cost of shipping them west, which meant that we had to lay out a measly eleven cents per case. And these were no seconds, but the same corn dogs you can buy in your favorite supermarket.

Donations keep flowing in. In fact, so many of our local farmers want to help out by providing us with acreage and crops that we are looking into starting our own production kitchen, where we could prepare some of our excess food to sell to other governmental bureaus and departments, from prisons to hospitals, at a cheaper rate than they could find elsewhere. In this way, we can generate some income and save even more money, while reducing expenditures at other government institutions as well.

Through all these measures (and also employing some skillful bartering, trading, and negotiating), we have cut the average cost of a meal by more than half, from sixty-five cents to approximately thirty cents, the least expensive meal in any sizable jail or prison system in the country. I'm talking about serving 25,000 meals each and every day (adding together adult and juvenile inmates). I'm talking about teaching 300 inmates to work in our kitchen, learning to handle food and cook and bake. I'm talking about providing two hot meals and one cold meal a day, all meals and menus approved by a county dietitian to ensure proper nutrition.

Our system works so well that we get calls from prison and jail systems from Maine to New York to California asking for advice and assistance in incorporating our programs into their plans and designs.

Not bad. Not bad at all.

So after all this talk about pasteurizing and farming and haggling, you're probably wondering exactly what the inmates eat. The *New York*

Post, in typical tabloid style, provided a day's menu, under the unblushing headline, "Yummy, yummy! Green bologna for the tummy."

"Breakfast: Cereal; tasteless and runny scrambled powdered eggs; leftover fruit gleaned from local farms by inmate labor; bread, and buttermilk.

"Lunch: Two white bread sandwiches, one green bologna, the other peanut butter; fruit; carrots; Kool-Aid.

"Dinner: A runny Sloppy Joe-like mixture with one slice of white bread, and a half-cooked potato; a wilted salad; Kool-Aid."

So judge for yourself. The menu might not be your idea of culinary delight, but then the odds are that if you're reading my book, you're probably not an inmate in my jail. I'm saving money while providing an officially approved, nutritional dietary plan for 6,000-plus prisoners. So where's the problem? What's the controversy?

I don't see any but sound management practices and a rational penal philosophy.

Oh, and about that bologna: It turns green when the meat isn't mixed exactly right, and the air gets in and oxidation occurs and colors appear and eureka!—you have green bologna, or maybe blue or purple or red. For some strange reason, everybody wants to talk about the bologna, from *The New York Times* to Tom Snyder, which just about scans the spectrum. (Tom, in particular, seemed to really get a kick out of the bologna. At the top of his show, before I was introduced, he stated that I was "said to be the toughest sheriff in America. This guy feeds the prisoners bologna sandwiches." Dramatic pause. "*Cold* bologna sandwiches." Pause. "*Green*, cold bologna sandwiches." And then Snyder and his off-camera audience broke up laughing.)

The media attention is okay by me as long as the reporters and the public understand the central point, which is, in a sentence: I will do what it takes to make my system work and work the best it can, effectively, efficiently, and within our budget. And if green bologna has somehow come to symbolize our efforts, well then, that's what symbols are for.

Making our jails tougher and better

So we continue to work on making our jails tougher and better. Inmates were smuggling in drugs and other contraband in their long hair, so everyone gets a haircut, the job done by other inmates, which turns out to both save money on professional barbers, and provide on-the-job vocational training. Network shows are out, and television viewing is restricted mostly to C-SPAN, ESPN, the Disney Channel, the Weather Channel and the local government access channel. I also pumped in Newt Gingrich's ten-part videotape series on revitalizing our American civilization. It seemed self-evident that the inmates could use as many lessons on good citizenship as they could get.

I'm still not exactly sure why, but my decision to show Newt Gingrich's tapes caused quite a media dustup. I had actually purchased the tapes, with inmates' funds, naturally, long before anybody in the press heard about it. So I was kind of surprised when a few journalists got wind of my video viewing plans, and this not-entirely-new, not-exactly-news story suddenly zoomed around the world.

Much of the media wasn't certain how to react. Some decided to express approval, a few went the other way, and many smartly opted to stick with being amused. I'll leave it to Rush Limbaugh, surely the most influential political commentator in America today, to explain what I did, and what I meant, as he told the story to his television audience, in the studio and throughout America:

"In addition to taking away coffee and other perks, he's decided to add the ten-part Newt Gingrich course on renewing American civilization. Is that not great?" The studio applauded as Rush beamed.

"Now here are a couple of fascinating quotes from Mr. Arpaio," Limbaugh said, "because of course . . . this is an engraved invitation to the ACLU to come give him trouble. In fact he says, 'I understand some people might call this cruel and unusual punishment, but so what?'"

The hard truth is that most of the prisoners are con men through and through.

Rush spoke over the applause. "All right! Now, my friends, get this one. He was asked, 'Well, wait a minute. So you've got Mr. Newt's ten-part video course that you're going to show on your ex-cable TV system. Don't you need to balance Mr. Newt with some Democratic tapes?' And he said, 'For one thing, I don't think there are any Democratic tapes. And some people might say these guys already got enough of their ideas anyway.'"

Laughter and applause resounded through the studio.

"But lest you think Sheriff Arpaio is political," said Rush, and he paused to give a big stage wink, "here's a little video clip of Mr. Arpaio so you can actually hear and see him yourself."

And Limbaugh showed a tape of me stating that I'd take anybody's video series, as long as it was good, including President Clinton's, if of course he had produced a sufficiently interesting program.

Rush ended his piece by staring at the camera and intoning, "You don't have to worry about that."

But enough about the tapes—back to the inmates: In the neverending attempt to procure favorable treatment, convicts were abusing the right to visit the nurse or doctor, so we instituted three dollar co-payments for inmate-initiated medical services. (If an inmate does not have three dollars, he will not be denied medical attention.) Inmates are subject to random drug testing, and the tactical squad periodically searches the jails for drugs, weapons, and other illegal or prohibited goods. Violation of the rules is punished by inmates being confined to lockdown, i.e., twenty-three hours out of every twenty-four in solitary. In addition, inmates who have been sentenced must work or go to lockdown.

The truth is, I don't think these measures are that tough, they're just common sense. However, unlike many of my political counterparts, I'm willing to actually implement these ideas and accept whatever consequences might come.

And let us not forget, if an inmate follows the rules and tries to make something of his life, he can study and get his high school equivalency or participate in a work assignment or gain some vocational training or get help with his substance-abuse problem. You see, even in jail, even in a very tough jail, an individual can learn and ponder and change and emerge a better human being.

Sadly, most do not make that choice. I know I've said it before, but it's worth saying again. Most—and I mean almost 70 percent—choose to learn nothing, choose to keep breaking the law, choose to keep returning to jail. If all those inmates who comprise that 70 percent are too stupid or corrupted or just plain vicious to go straight for their own good or the good of their families, then maybe my jails will convince a few, or maybe more than a few, to obey the law and get an honest job just to stay out of the tents and away from the green bologna.

A visiting reporter from a Minneapolis television station found and interviewed an inmate who also hailed from Minnesota, and the convict's feeling about his experience in the Maricopa County jails warmed my heart: "It's going to deter me from coming back to Arizona, that's for sure. I'm going back home, and I ain't coming back!"

I regularly visit my jails, talking to the prisoners and the officers. I listen to their complaints and their problems. The hard truth is that most of the prisoners are con men through and through. They walk up to you and look you in the eye and say they never did anything, that this is one big mistake or conspiratorial frame. All they want to do is get out and be the upstanding, outstanding citizens they really are. And, finally, inevitably, invariably, can you help them out with—select one or more—the guards, the courts, the parole board, the mayor, the governor, the Pope, you name it.

Forget the social workers. Forget the shrinks. Forget the ACLU. That's the way it really is. Those are the kind of people you're usually really dealing with. Given all that, there's only so much you can do, only so much you can really hope to accomplish in the way of rehabilitation.

So, save the ones you can save. Help the ones you can help. Control the rest.

You don't like that word? Then how about manage or check or intimidate? Take your pick. Just get the job done, within the bounds of ethics and law.

Save the ones you can save. Help the ones you can help. Control the rest.

That might sound harsh to you. I don't know. If it sounds harsh, that's all right, because jail is a harsh place. Jail is not a reward or an achievement, it is punishment.

Amazingly, much of society seems to have forgotten that unvarnished reality.

If you've ever visited my jails, tent or hard facility variety, you know I haven't forgotten. I promise the people I never will.

2

Violent Offenders Should Be Placed in Supermax Prisons

California Department of Corrections

The California Department of Corrections operates all state prisons, oversees several community correctional facilities, and supervises all parolees during their re-entry into society.

Pelican Bay State Prison houses California's most secure prison facility—the Security Housing Unit (SHU), a "supermax" prison. This is where the most violent and dangerous prisoners are housed. In order to ensure the safety of inmates and staff, prisoners in the SHU experience solitary confinement, limited movement, little or no contact with others, and strictly controlled leisure time. This results in a successful program that punishes offenders and keeps violence to a minimum.

California's most secure prison facility—the high-tech Security Housing Unit (SHU)—is located within the maximum custody Pelican Bay State Prison. Its purpose: to protect staff and male inmates throughout the system from the few most violent, predatory offenders.

The prison is geographically isolated, lying just south of the Oregon border near the coastal community of Crescent City, California. One side of the prison houses maximum custody inmates in general population—those who can hold jobs, go to school and mingle with other inmates.

Those assigned to Pelican Bay's SHU (pronounced shoo) have none of these privileges. They have proven by their behavior in prison that they cannot be housed safely with general population inmates.

The 1,056-bed facility at Pelican Bay is one of two Security Housing Units the department currently operates. The other, a 512-bed facility at Corcoran State Prison, houses both SHU and protective custody inmates.

Earning a trip to SHU

Not every inmate is "eligible" for SHU. Most are sent there for committing violent acts while in prison such as murder, assault, initiating

Reprinted, with permission, from "Pelican Bay State Prison Security Housing Unit," a brochure published by the California Department of Corrections.

a riot, threatening staff or other inmates, or being caught with a weapon. An administrative review committee considers the evidence and listens to the inmate and witnesses. If the charges are verified, inmates can be given a SHU term ranging from a few months to five years.

Known gang members and affiliates—especially those responsible for violence or intimidation within the prison—also can be assigned to SHU. Because there is no set term for gang members assigned to SHU, the department conducts a thorough investigation to document the inmate's gang activities and reviews his status every 120 days.

Designed for maximum protection

Pelican Bay's SHU often is referred to as a "super-max" prison. It was designed to ensure the maximum protection for inmates and staff.

Most inmates are in single cells. Heavy, perforated cell doors limit an inmate's ability to assault others, without obstructing visibility into or out of a cell. Bunks are molded into the wall and toilets have no removable parts that could be used to make weapons. All clothing, bedding and personal effects are x-rayed before being placed in a cell. There are eight individual cells in each pod. A shower is located on each floor. Several overhead skylights flood each pod with natural light. Each pod has its own 26' by 10' exercise yard.

The pods are arranged in a semi-circle, like spokes of a wheel, with a centralized control room as the hub. The control room officer has a clear view of all six pods, also called cell blocks. The officer operates each door, controls the entrances and exits to each pod, and monitors movement in the exercise yards via closed circuit television.

The SHU complex encompasses both housing and support functions within a single building envelope. A secure system of corridors is monitored by control rooms. To aid in the secure operation of the complex, the upper level corridors are restricted to staff only. Heavy mesh grating on the floor of the upper corridor allows close scrutiny of activity below.

Controlling inmate movement

Most SHU inmates are allowed a limited amount of unescorted movement within the pod. For example, an inmate can walk alone from his cell to the shower or to the exercise yard. This reduces the frequency of physical contact between staff and inmates and greatly diminishes the risk of assault. Only one inmate at a time is allowed to move within the pod.

Before an inmate moves outside his pod, he is placed in restraints. He is escorted to secure areas within the SHU complex by two correctional officers. He may:

- Receive health services
- Meet with counseling or administrative staff
- Conduct legal research
- Attend classification, parole or disciplinary hearings
- Visit with family or friends (non-contact visits only)

Minimizing inmate-to-inmate contact

One way of controlling violence within a prison is to minimize the physical contact inmates have with one another. Unlike other institutions where lower custody inmates provide support services, at Pelican Bay's SHU only staff have physical contact with inmates.

Staff in the housing unit deliver food trays, mail, canteen supplies, or medications. In the law library they process requests for information, transmit approved material between inmates, and deliver reference books. Those few SHU inmates who share a cell can exercise together. Otherwise, the inmates are kept separate from one another throughout the prison.

Inmates from the Level IV side of the institution do come into the building to prepare meals, operate the canteen, or assist with routine maintenance. These general population inmates are searched when they come and go, are closely supervised while inside, and are kept separate from those housed there. They also wear special jumpsuits to distinguish them from SHU inmates.

By enforcing this kind of separation, the prison eliminates the possibility that inmates can be used as go-betweens for information or contraband. Further, it ensures that no inmate has a position of greater status or access within the SHU.

Providing inmate health care

Each SHU facility offers a full range of health care services including emergency care, routine medical diagnosis and treatment, mental health consultation, and dental care.

Pelican Bay's SHU . . . was designed to ensure the maximum protection for inmates and staff.

In many instances, physicians can diagnose and treat inmates during their "rounds" to the housing units. Most medications are dispensed on site by medical technicians.

Any inmate needing complex medical treatment, dental care or in-depth psychological counseling is escorted in restraints to the infirmary. If the problem is beyond the scope of the prison infirmary, the inmate will be transported to a community hospital for treatment. The prison provides round-the-clock security for any inmates removed from the institution.

Accommodating legal research

SHU inmates are allowed reasonable access to the prison law library for research. Run by an accredited librarian, Pelican Bay's library maintains up-to-date legal texts and research materials.

Inmates schedule library time in advance. Small groups are escorted to the library then locked into individual cells for study. The court has ruled that inmates may share legal materials with each other. Security staff search the material for contra-band or unauthorized messages before they make the transfer.

One way of controlling violence within a prison is to minimize the physical contact inmates have with one another.

The law library is designed to allow inmates time for quiet study. However, a court decision also allows conversation between inmates in library cells.

Making use of leisure time

Because of the high security level of the SHU, all leisure time activities are strictly controlled.

Visiting—Family members and friends can visit SHU inmates on regularly scheduled visiting days. All visits are non-contact visits. The inmate is escorted into a small, secure cell. The visitor sits on the opposite side of a Plexiglas divider and communicates with the inmate via telephone.

Exercise—Inmates have access to the exercise yard at least 10 hours per week. For security reasons, no exercise equipment is allowed. The concrete exercise area measures 10' wide by 26' long by 18' high. One half of the top is covered with Plexiglas for protection during inclement weather. The other half is open to the air but covered with a heavy mesh screen. Video cameras mounted at either end of the yard allow constant surveillance of the inmate's movements by the control room officer inside.

Religion—Religious services and programs are offered to SHU inmates on an individual basis. Chaplains meet with inmates in the housing unit or at the cell door.

Entertainment—Inmates may have radios and television sets inside their cells. They must use earphones to listen to the programs.

3

Strict Discipline Lowers Prison Violence

Christopher Drew

Christopher Drew is a reporter for the New York Times. *He writes on a vast array of subjects, including politics and criminal justice.*

Rikers Island in New York is a prison that was once known for violence and riots. However, in five short years, Mayor Rudolph Giuliani of New York and others have cracked down on prisoner violence and made Rikers safer. New supervisors have instituted no-nonsense control devices such as pepper spray and stun guns. New technology allows guards to search for contraband more thoroughly than ever before. The strict program has lowered violence and inmate attacks substantially, creating a safer environment for both guards and prisoners.

Just five years after city officials braced for riots on Rikers Island, where inmates routinely slit each other with razors, gangs were a menace and guards brawled with inmates in a perpetual fight for control, violence inside the sprawling complex of city jails has been brought to extraordinary lows.

Using an array of tools and tactics—from a huge S.W.A.T. team to electric stun shields to a program that aggressively prosecutes inmates for crimes committed inside the jails—correction officials have reduced slashings and stabbings among inmates by more than 90 percent. Stabbing assaults by inmates have plummeted to 78 so far this year [1999] from nearly 1,100 in 1994.

This aggressive effort has radically changed the climate inside jails that were notoriously chaotic and brutal, and where both inmates and guards were fearful.

"Now, it's a different ballgame," Bernard B. Kerik, the city's Commissioner of Correction, said. "I tell you, if somebody had told my officers five years ago we'd ever get the violence down this low, they would have laughed in your face."

The changes have not come without concerns. Some inmates and their legal advocates view the new tactics, particularly the use of pepper gas and stun devices to subdue inmates, with alarm. They say there have been several cases of dangerous abuse, and they contend that jail officials have been weak in disciplining guards.

"There is no question that it is easier to control the inmates," said Jonathan S. Chasan, a lawyer for the Prisoners' Rights Project at the Legal Aid Society. But, he added, "Whenever you impose a system of restraint on this scale, it can easily be abused."

Still, judging from interviews with guards, inmates and lawyers for some of the 17,000 people who at any moment are awaiting trial on Rikers or in other detention houses, there is a general perception that the jails have been made safer and more manageable.

Zero tolerance

To supporters and critics of the crackdown, the effort at Rikers is a case of the [mayor of New York City, Rudolph W.] Giuliani administration's enforcing its zero-tolerance approach to crime in its rawest form, and correction officials from Maryland, Florida and Connecticut have examined the program as a kind of model.

The sense of safety taking hold at Rikers has been achieved through an ambitious, unapologetic program employing everything from high-tech weaponry to common sense.

The stun devices—large plexiglass shields threaded with wires—deliver six-second bursts of 50,000 volts of electricity, and are used to incapacitate inmates and cut the risk of hand-to-hand violence. The devices, which crackle and spark when held against an inmate, have been used 74 times, or about once a week, since they were deployed a year and a half ago. Mace or pepper spray has been used 1,500 times over the last three and a half years.

While controversial, both the spray and the stun devices are increasingly being used in jails and prisons around the country, and New York City health officials have approved their use against inmates who are generally healthy. Mr. Kerik, 44, a hard-edged former policeman, said he remained willing to try anything else that seemed likely to cut the violence further.

That attitude, some visitors say, has led to changes that have replaced a bloody hot-house atmosphere in some cellblocks with an almost eerie, "Twilight Zone" calm.

At Mr. Kerik's suggestion, inmates who have slashed others now walk around with their hands clamped inside foot-long protective tubes, known as "the mitts." During cellblock raids, guards often bring in chairs with magnetic sensors that can search for bits of metal hidden in inmates' mouths and other body cavities.

Another crucial change has been the creation of a jail intelligence unit, which has disrupted the gangs and increased arrests of inmates.

In the past, most people who punched a guard or were caught with weapons were simply shifted to a disciplinary ward. But over the last two years, more than 1,800 inmates have been arrested and charged with new crimes for violent acts and jail infractions.

Inmates themselves say the threat of additional jail time has become a powerful deterrent.

Rodney Morris was held on Rikers for two years before being acquitted last month on murder charges. He also had been there before, in 1990.

"Back then," he said, "it was more of a convict jail, where people were getting cut more and robbed more."

But, he said, "that's not happening now, because basically, the brothers know that if I cut somebody, I will get arrested. And one thing the brothers are not trying to do is get more jail time."

Days of chaos, blood, and reprisal

When Kevin Butler became a correction officer at Rikers in the early 1980's, emergency alarms sometimes signaled serious confrontations with inmates 10 times a day.

And until recently, he said, "You could never be comfortable in the jails, because at any second it could be chaos in this place."

Rikers has also been more difficult to control than most jails and prisons. Unlike the convicts in federal and state custody, most inmates in the city's jails are detainees, legally innocent and awaiting trial, and more than 125,000 men and women cycle through each year. Many also are habitual criminals or drug abusers, and are prone to lash out.

Hundreds of officers and inmates were hurt in riots in the late 1980's and in 1990. But just as corrosive were the dozens of daily conflicts over simple complaints about food or recreation time, any of which could quickly turn violent or touch off a melee in a cellblock. As the jails began to fill with members of gangs like the Latin Kings and the Bloods, the violence got even more cut-throat.

Inmates were armed with metal yanked from mops and radiators, plexiglass from light fixtures and bits of razor blades melted into the handles of toothbrushes. Some threw urine or feces on guards or reached out to slash officers as they walked by.

Meanwhile, the Correction Department was reeling, its ranks thinning from a freeze on hiring in the early 1990's and its leadership overwhelmed. Wardens took to shuffling the worst inmates back and forth to one another's jails under the guise of relieving overcrowding. Some of the guards took it upon themselves to restore order.

Records from lawsuits show that when inmates were sent to the disciplinary ward, they often received "greeting beatings." At other times, jail supervisors ordered assaults on antagonistic inmates. Serious head injuries and broken bones were common.

And when Mayor Rudolph W. Giuliani began to trim drug treatment services in late 1994, riots looked possible, prompting city officials to finally try to change the vicious dynamics on the island.

New leadership, tough tactics

As a first step, Mr. Giuliani replaced the leadership of the Correction Department. A former city budget official, Michael P. Jacobson, became the commissioner, and Mr. Kerik got the No. 2 job, overseeing day-to-day operations.

Mr. Kerik, a blunt, irrepressible man, had once been a $52,000-a-year jail warden in Passaic County, N.J. But when he got a chance to fulfill a lifelong dream, and become a New York City policeman, he grabbed it, taking a $25,000 pay cut.

During eight years with the Police Department, Mr. Kerik won 30 medals, including the Medal of Valor for a shootout in which he wounded a drug dealer who had shot Mr. Kerik's partner. He also grew a ponytail and wore five diamond earrings as an undercover drug operative.

To Mr. Kerik, fixing the crisis in the jails simply called for street smarts. "People at first thought I was crazy," he said.

But Mr. Jacobson also was willing to experiment. And what emerged was an unusual patchwork of changes, some off the cuff and others tested at length, all meant to limit the chances for violence.

Jails have been made safer and more manageable.

One of Mr. Kerik's first ideas was to start handcuffing inmates behind their backs rather than with their hands in front. He was upset that some had hidden razor blades in their mouths, retrieving them with their cuffed hands to attack inmates and guards.

Later, after he read about the protective tubes in a trade magazine, he ordered their use over handcuffs to immobilize the most dangerous inmates outside their cells.

Other simple changes included a ban on sneakers with air cushions, because inmates were hiding razor blades in them. Even the size of the food-tray openings on some cells has been trimmed to stop inmates from swiping at passing guards.

Mr. Kerik, who became the commissioner in early 1998 after Mr. Jacobson resigned, said jail officials also had to show the inmates they were no longer afraid of them—and that they had the tools to clamp down without resorting to their fists.

Thus the department has spent $13 million to increase security. It has created a 111-member S.W.A.T. team to halt major riots and a Gang Intelligence Unit to monitor the roughly 2,000 gang members who are in the jails at any time. And it turned to the gas and the stun shields.

Jail supervisors and some guards carry canisters of pepper spray. The department also bought 90 stun shields for $545 apiece.

The shields and the spray are mainly used when teams go into a cell to subdue inmates who have misbehaved or who refuse to step out during a search—a type of confrontation that has often led to injuries among inmates and guards.

Jail officials said just the threat of the devices was often enough to persuade inmates to comply. But if an inmate starts to fight, Mr. Kerik said, one officer can spray the gas or ram the shield into the inmate, disorienting him while the other guards put on handcuffs. "This has really prevented a lot of injuries," he said.

These days, the chair means something else

Early one recent afternoon, 30 correction officers poured into a maximum-security cellblock at the James A. Thomas Center, the island's most forbidding jail.

Emmanuel H. Bailey, an assistant deputy warden who heads the Gang Intelligence Unit, which makes all the arrests on the island, was with them. Fifteen members of the S.W.A.T. team waited in the hall.

Wearing latex gloves, the officers rummaged through the cells, each containing a toilet, sink, a few shelves and a metal bed. The inmates stood outside their cells, waiting to run their mattresses through X-ray machines like the ones in airports.

Then the focus turned to a speckled gray chair that has done as much as anything to calm the mood of the place. One by one, the inmates filed over to it, each placing his chin, followed by his left cheek and then his right cheek, on a tall oval platform at the top. Then they climbed into the seat.

The chair, made of pressed wood, contains magnetic sensors. Jail officials say it has allowed them to do what was almost impossible before—to search for weapons stashed within the inmates' bodies.

For years, inmates have wrapped razor blades, bobby pins and metal shanks in toilet paper or matchbook covers, tied strings around them, and hid them down their throats or in their body cavities. This was dangerous, of course. But it was also one of the main reasons it was so hard to rid the jails of weapons.

But now the device, called the Body Orifice Scanning System, or B.O.S.S. chair, is wheeled in during searches. "And if somebody's got a weapon, it is going to let us know," Mr. Bailey said.

During this search, the chair's signal lights never flashed. The only razor blade to turn up was in an air-conditioning vent.

Indeed, since jail officials intensified the raids, weapon recoveries have dropped sharply, from 9,329 in fiscal 1997 to 5,122 in the year that ended in June [1998 to 1999], indicating that many inmates no longer want to risk being caught with them.

As the search neared an end, Mr. Bailey and two of his deputies stepped forward to arrest an inmate who had been caught earlier trying to hide a balloon of crack cocaine in his rectum.

Weapon recoveries have dropped sharply . . . indicating that many inmates no longer want to risk being caught with them.

"If you leave like a gentleman, we won't have any problems," Mr. Bailey said.

Mr. Bailey said later that in the past, inmates might easily have been jeering and throwing garbage during a search.

But nobody misbehaved. Only one inmate even bothered to look angry.

That inmate, a muscular 28-year-old man, said in an interview that the guard searching his cell had torn a religious calendar and scattered his legal papers.

"It's already a demoralizing environment," he said. "Why do they have to make it worse?"

But another inmate, Deshawn Sealy, 22, who had a ready smile and a Bible on his table, said he was pleased with the protection. Mr. Sealy said he had been arrested for fighting near his home in the South Bronx, and that he tried to keep to himself at Rikers.

"A lot of the other guys have razor blades and stuff like that, and a person like myself can get hurt," he said.

Concerns arise on inmates' rights

To inmate advocates and other critics, some of the changes at Rikers are justified, but others seem overzealous, including aspects of the effort to prosecute inmates for crimes committed inside the jails.

No one questions that inmates who commit serious crimes should get additional jail time, and perhaps the most striking instance involves Kowwani Brunstorf.

Last fall [1998], Mr. Brunstorf was acquitted on the murder charge that had led him to Rikers. But while he was in jail, he had sliced another inmate, attempted to slash an officer and wrestled a jail supervisor to the ground. So after pleading guilty in March to charges arising from those incidents, he was sentenced to six and a half to eight years and sent to Attica.

Otherwise, "he'd be home right now," said his lawyer, Edward D. Wilford.

City records show that other inmates have received sentences of three months to several years for possessing weapons or starting fires, including some set as protests just before they bailed themselves out of jail on other charges.

But some inmates and their lawyers are concerned that over the last two years, more than 700 of the 1,800 arrests of inmates have been for assaulting guards.

"I think a number of the arrests are questionable," said John Boston, the director of the Prisoners' Rights Project at the Legal Aid Society.

He said it was easy for guards to cover up their own brutality by pressing assault charges against those who fight back.

The concerns about abuses also extend to the use of the pepper gas and stun shields.

The manufacturers of the implements insist that they do not cause permanent harm. But Christine M. Doyle, an attorney for Amnesty International U.S.A., said both the gas and the shields were dehumanizing, and other kinds of stun technology, like stun belts and guns, have been used for torture.

She also said that while more than 130 jail and prison systems now use stun devices, there have been serious injuries in other jurisdictions.

Before using either the spray or the shields, guards at Rikers are required to check with the jails' medical department to determine which inmates have heart conditions or other problems that could be aggravated. Any use of those devices is also supposed to be videotaped.

Jonathan S. Chasan, a Legal Aid lawyer, said that at least three inmates with asthma had been sprayed even though that is prohibited by jail rules. One of the inmates, James Hill, has sued the city, saying he had to spend two weeks in a hospital because of irritations to his lungs.

Mr. Chasan said some of the officers in the cases he cited were not disciplined, while one was docked only a vacation day as punishment. Mr. Kerik said that every incident is investigated, and some rules have been changed to prevent recurrences. In another case, he said, one officer who had sprayed an inmate who threw wet toilet paper at him lost eight vacation days, which would be worth $1,400 to $1,500 in pay.

"I am confident that that sends a pretty clear message," Mr. Kerik added.

And in pushing ahead with the new techniques, jail officials also have the support of the City Board of Correction, an agency that sets minimum standards for the treatment of inmates.

The board's chairman, John R. Horan, said he was "not crazy" about the stun shields. But he said the board had given "a cautious O.K." to their use. "They are potentially dangerous," he said. "But it also is dangerous for officers to have to deal with inmates when they 'act out' violently."

The guards, to be sure, are grateful for the extra firepower.

Sean Maynard, a correction officer, said: "It shows we're in charge."

4

Working Prisoners Benefit the Economy

Morgan O. Reynolds

Morgan O. Reynolds is the director of the Criminal Justice Center for the National Center for Policy Analysis as well as a professor of economics at Texas A&M University.

The inmate population in America's prisons stands today at over 1.1 million and continues to grow at an enormous rate. Society should put prisoners to work for the private sector so that their labor can be used productively. Prison labor creates new jobs outside the prison system, lightens taxpayer burdens, and encourages innovation in the private sector—the key to economic growth. Policy reforms need to be enacted now so that America can take advantage of this untapped resource.

My name is Morgan O. Reynolds and I am Director of the Criminal Justice Center at the Dallas-based National Center for Policy Analysis and a professor of economics at Texas A&M University in College Station, Texas. I would like to thank Chairman Henry J. Hyde and the Judiciary's Subcommittee on Crime for asking me to testify today on the economics of prison industry.

The cost of operating the nation's prisons is soaring, along with the number of people in prisons.

Since 1980 the state and federal prison population has increased from 316,000 to 1.1 million.

By the year 2002 the inmate population is expected to increase by another 43 percent.

The expense has reached about $25 billion a year, or $250 a year for every household in America.

One of the most obvious proposals to reduce the cost of criminal justice is to increase the amount of productive work by prisoners. Yet, despite a longstanding consensus in favor of gainful employment for convicts, idleness remains the norm in prison.

Over the years, federal and state laws, often to appease those opposed to competition from prison made goods, have denied convicts opportunities

Reprinted from "The Economics of Prison Industries: The Products of Our Prison," testimony given by Morgan O. Reynolds before the Subcommittee on Crime, Committee on the Judiciary, U.S. House of Representatives, Washington, D.C., September 13, 1996.

for productive employment. Half seriously, perhaps we need a national "right to work" law for convicts. Halting steps have been taken to permit the sale of prison made goods in the marketplace and to create private sector jobs for prisoners, but legal restrictions, aided by bureaucratic inertia and labor union sensitivities, continue to hamper progress.

In 1985, the late Chief Justice Warren E. Burger urged repeal of all statutes limiting prison production and discriminating against prison made goods. Burger urged the cooperation of business and organized labor to use prison labor productively. Burger proposed an immediate increase in the number of prisoners working from 10 percent of the prison population to 20 percent, with a 10 year goal of "a full 50 percent of inmates working." More than 10 years later, Burger's proposed goal is no closer than it was then.

Why the private sector needs to be involved

States need only so many license plates, so much furniture for government agencies and so many workers harvesting radishes on prison farms. Thus the private sector must be involved both in creating jobs and in finding markets for prison made products if prisoner work is ever to employ large numbers of inmates and produce significant income.

Prisoners employed by the private sector, whether by contract or lease, historically out-produced those working in public prison industries by substantial margins. In 1885 revenues as a percentage of operating cost were at least 100 percent for convict leases to private entrepreneurs and farmers, 62 percent for contract labor inside prisons, 32 percent for state run prison industries, and 18 percent for piece price contracts. As penologist Howard Gill wrote in 1931, "It appears that idleness increases as public control increases."

Projected gains for taxpayers

In a survey by the Enterprise Prison Institute, prison industry managers frequently mentioned 25 percent of prisoners as a desired target for employment. Governor Tommy Thompson of Wisconsin has set a goal of 25 percent of state prisoners privately employed. U.S. Senator Phil Gramm (R., TX) has proposed that federal prisoners pay 50 percent of their annual support through prison work.

If one in four prisoners could be put to work for private enterprise . . . taxpayer costs would fall by $2.4 billion per year.

What could we reasonably expect under an aggressive expansion of private production by prisoners? If one in four prisoners could be put to work for private enterprise over the next five to 10 years, that implies about 400,000 new prison jobs, a 3/1,000th increase in the American workforce spread over many years. Such a small increase in the work force could not have a serious competitive impact unless most of the labor was concentrated on a handful of products. Taxpayer costs would fall by $2.4 billion per year, or nearly 10 percent of the cost of prisons.

One of the difficulties of creating jobs for prisoners is that many of them are illiterate or semiliterate, or have low IQs, yet champions of inmate labor are confident such jobs could be created. The federal system may have the best prospects for high rates of payback because many of the prisoners are there for crimes typically committed by more intelligent criminals, such as counterfeiting, kidnapping and drug smuggling.

There are both economic and rehabilitative advantages to having prisoners work. Revenue from prisoner produced goods and services can offset part or all of the cost of incarceration. Part of the wages paid to prisoners can be used for taxes and go to victims for restitution, and to the prisoners' families for upkeep. Under the current system, the lack of productive prison jobs has limited efforts to gain restitution for victims. A typical set of deductions from a prisoner's wages would be 20 percent each for room and board, taxes and victim compensation, and 10 percent each for legal obligations, savings, family support and personal consumption.

Benefits to prisoners

Putting prisoners to work at productive jobs results in better behaved prisoners, and can help train prisoners in work habits and skills and increase the likelihood of a productive life when they are released.

Prisoners overwhelmingly prefer work to the tedium of prison life. This is common knowledge among experts. Prisoners especially value opportunities to work for private sector firms, as is demonstrated by the number who sign up for prison industry jobs wherever formal waiting lists exist.

Prisoners who work behave better. This is confirmed by prison officials, although hard data from social scientists are less abundant and more controversial. For example, a 1989 survey found mixed results. However, a federal Post Release Employment Project (PREP) study confirms that employed prisoners do better both inside and outside of prison than those who do not work. Data was collected from 1983 to 1987 on more than 7,000 federal offenders. Participants were less likely to have a misconduct report during their last year of incarceration and when they did receive a misconduct report it was less likely to have been serious. Only 6.6 percent of those who worked in prison had their parole revoked or were charged with committing a new crime during their first year of supervised release, compared to 10.1 percent of the group who had not worked in prison. Prison work and training programs seem to have been especially effective in reducing the likelihood of recidivism in the long term.

Badger State Industries (BSI), Wisconsin's state prison industries program, employs about 600 of Wisconsin's 10,000 prisoners to produce everything from coffee cups to furniture. A study indicates that the recidivism rate after three years was 15 percent lower for those who worked for BSI than for those who did not. According to BSI's director, Steve Kronzer, "People who worked for prison industries tended to do better than normal."

Restricting work by prisoners

Allied with prison reformers, interest groups eventually succeeded in many cases in obtaining restrictive legislation against what they regarded as unfair low wage competition. Prison wardens, fearing a loss of decision making power and the new task of supervising unproductive and idle prisoners, vigorously opposed new restrictions. Ironically, prison workshops generally had a hard time competing with private enterprise. Nevertheless, because it involved convicted felons and because questions were sometimes raised about the terms on which prisons awarded contracts to entrepreneurs, the "prison industry had certain attributes which made it a convenient scapegoat for the troubles of working men."

Putting prisoners to work at productive jobs results in better behaved prisoners.

As a result of restrictions by the federal and state governments, "the original conception of the penitentiary was thus turned on its head," Andrew Peyton Thomas, a young assistant attorney general in Arizona, said recently. "Prison labor, once viewed as indispensable for restoring a healthy relationship between the criminal and society, was made literally a federal offense." The irony is that "whether their preferred penal philosophy was rehabilitation, retribution or deterrence, virtually all of the founders of America's prisons believed in the values of prison labor."

Today's renewed interest in prison labor stems from the tremendous increases in the prisoner population, the diminished belief that prisons can reform prisoners and an American business community unafraid of competition from labor intensive products best suited to prisons and typically produced offshore. Progress has been slow, both because of the PIE program's many constraints and because increasing work for convicts has not had a high priority with either government officials or private sector businesses.

Answering the critics

Objections to competition from prison made products were largely responsible for the restrictive state and federal laws that play a big part in the idleness of so many prisoners today. Are these objections and concerns serious enough to keep productive work for prisoners to a minimum? No, they can be dealt with in ways that allow the vastly expanded use of this resource.

From an economist's perspective, newly created value whether produced inside or outside prisons is a social boon, not a curse. Production by prisoners creates rather than destroys jobs, systemwide. For example, if prisoners make filing cabinets, the task requires someone to manufacture sheet metal, to transport it to the worksite and to transport the finished product. These and the demands for many other goods and services create new jobs. Prison idleness, not activity, has silently eradicated demand for the outputs of freeworld workers.

Certain firms and local labor, to be sure, might be hurt more than helped by prison production, at least in the short run. Yet remember that the number of jobs is unlimited since more jobs exist at lower compensation rates. Contrary to prevailing myth, there cannot be a shortage of jobs if labor suppliers can accept lower wage rates. In the world of scarcity in which we live, there is an infinite amount of work to do and more production is welcomed by consumers and businesses. The real issue is economic growth and its attendant rising productivity and wages.

In the competitive fray, one person's productive success can indirectly harm or even ruin a competing supplier financially. Yet we tolerate competition, even celebrate it, because its advantages vastly outweigh its disadvantages. Despite sometimes visible and poignant costs, competition is good rather than bad. As gymnastics coach Bela Karolyi put it, "No competition, no progress." Economist Joseph Schumpeter (1883–1950) called the innovations that render obsolete old inventories, ideas, technologies, skills and equipment "gales of creative destruction." The only alternative to consumer sovereignty and free markets is producer sovereignty and guaranteed monopoly. This would serve us very badly as a society because only competition allows us to discover the cheapest and most efficient or effective way to do any job, thus freeing up productive resources for new tasks.

Consider a related issue: welfare reform. Getting able-bodied adults off welfare and into jobs is widely viewed as progress rather than as a threat to the livelihood of others. Work for prisoners, by contrast, has been treated as a competitive threat. What is the economic difference? None, really. To be sure, community hostility toward convicts emerges from the fact that they are criminals, and welfare recipients are merely dependents. Yet there is little concern (properly) over the competitive impact of large numbers of welfare recipients going to work. With 15 million persons receiving Aid to Families with Dependent Children, 6 million receiving Supplemental Security Income, 27.5 million on food stamps and millions more on Medicaid and other welfare programs, the potential impact of a large expansion in work and production among welfare recipients in an economy of 125 million jobs dwarfs that of putting fewer than one million prisoners to work.

Prison labor is primarily a complement rather than a competing substitute for the American labor force.

Fear of prison production resembles the debate over the so-called dumping of goods by foreign producers. Economists argue that we should let foreigners "dump" all the valuable goods they want. If others wish to give us their goods they add to the opportunity and wealth in our community. Adversely impacted business owners and displaced workers are seldom so sanguine. Yet, interest groups like the U.S. Chamber of Commerce and the AFL-CIO [The American Federation of Labor-Congress of Industrial Organizations—a federation of American unions] are on record in general support of private-sector prison industries.

Minimizing adverse impacts

Prison labor is primarily a complement rather than a competing substitute for the American labor force. Where substitution and job displacement is threatened, one way to minimize the adverse impact is to apply prison labor to products that have negligible domestic competitive effects. For example, Prison Blues, jeans produced by Oregon state prisoners, compete primarily with jeans produced offshore. A drawback is that if domestic, free private enterprise can't produce something at a profit, prison labor often can't, either. A second way to diminish local impact is to remove restrictions on prison made goods in interstate commerce, insuring that prison made products compete in a national market.

States and the federal government should repeal requirements that prison manufactured goods be used by government agencies or given preferences by those agencies. The federal government should do the same with its mandatory purchase requirement for federal agencies. This would give private enterprise enormously expanded opportunities to compete for the business of state and federal agencies and the new joint ventures employing prisoners.

Focusing only on wages can be misleading. There are many other factors that make prison production more, not less, expensive than non-prison production. These factors include security problems, high turnover, lack of skills, poor work habits and remote prison locations. A large percentage of inmates are illiterate or semiliterate. Prison labor usually is only suitable for labor intensive, low-skilled work, at least on a large scale. In general, profit is no more easily achieved in prison than out. If convict labor is cheaper than civilian labor, it is because the entrepreneur hiring the labor expects it to be less productive.

State and federal prison systems control a huge asset, convict labor and largely waste its productive potential. All 50 states now have prison industry programs, and in 1934 Federal Prison Industries, Inc. (trade name UNICOR) was established as a self-sustaining corporation to keep federal inmates constructively employed and provide job training. But the possibility of making a profit must be allowed if the rapidly growing population of prisoners is going to have gainful employment. This means repealing state and federal obstacles and encouraging private sector involvement.

Public policy reforms

Among the steps that need to be taken are these:
- Repeal the Sumners-Ashurst Act making it a federal crime to knowingly transport convict made goods in interstate commerce.
- Repeal the Walsh-Healy Act ban on the use of convict labor in federal procurement contracts over $10,000.
- Repeal similar state laws restricting trade in prison made goods and services.
- Repeal state use laws that compel state agencies to buy goods and services made in that state's prisons, and institute competitive bidding for all state, local and federal purchases.
- Repeal state and federal limitations on inmate pay to allow more flexible, market determined prices for inmates' labor (compensation based on anticipated productivity).
- Pay modest bonuses to wardens and prison officials for progress toward making their prisons financially self-sufficient.
- Create prison enterprise marketing offices in prison and jail systems.
- Allow private prison operators to profit from the gainful employment of convict labor.
- Encourage and publicize private sector proposals for enterprise prisons.

- Set up procedures for competitive bidding for prison labor. Diminish prisoner litigation against prison work by repealing the Civil Rights of Institutionalized Persons Act and the federal habeas corpus procedure and then institute the English rule by which prisoners can lose as well as gain something of value in lawsuits.
- Explicitly allow contracts for convict leasing for work outside prisons with responsible private enterprises, paying careful attention to legal liability, security against escape and state inspection and supervision.
- Reallocate effort away from makework training programs and nonprofit "doing good" and toward getting real jobs done.

Running prisons as a business

The proper way to mimic the free world of work as closely as possible is to encourage profit and loss employment of prison labor by private enterprise. Prisoner run firms might even be allowed, provided the activity is consistent with orderly operation of the facility.

The advantages to society of prison jobs vastly outweigh any disadvantages.

Inmates are eager to work for a variety of reasons: to relieve monotony, to earn money wages, to claim good time credit and early release. What about prisoner wages? Let them be flexible and set competitively. Prisoners and prison labor pools expected to yield low value added will attract low offers and vice versa for high value. The evidence shows that for products that need entry-level, unskilled workers who are reliable and stable (light mechanical assembly, welding, sorting, data entry, etc.), inmates can be competent, given close supervision and clear work standards. We can put many of the problems of prison industry into better competitive hands.

Policy options

Repeal of federal restrictions on prison labor would allow the states to design their own lease systems. Conditions and criteria would differ among the states. Some states could lease labor to industries both inside and outside prisons and retain final control, inspection and auditing responsibilities. Historically, private jobs in prisons diminished states with more trade unions and more concentrated employment in manufacturing. Allowing state authorities maximum latitude in negotiating prison lease deals would benefit taxpayers, prisoners and crime victims and would improve public safety over the long run. As the *Houston Chronicle* put it in a recent editorial, "The advantages to society of prison jobs vastly outweigh any disadvantages."

Comprehensive legislation from the Congress is important because a coherent package would make the goals and methods clear and elevate the visibility and caliber of political discussion. More gainful work for prisoners would overwhelmingly benefit American taxpayers, crime victims, consumers, workers and investors.

5

Jail: Rough Road or Easy Street?

Dana Tofig

Dana Tofig writes for the Connecticut-based Hartford Courant, *the nation's oldest newspaper. She has written about other prison topics such as aging in prison.*

In recent years, the public has grown increasingly intolerant of crime, which has led to calls for fewer amenities in prisons. However, according to prison officials, recreational and educational programs help break up the monotony of prison life and relieve the stress that can result in prison violence. Politicians and "get-tough-on-prisoners" advocates like Sheriff Joe Arpaio of Arizona recommend the elimination of perks because it makes them popular with the voters. But what they do not realize is that if amenities in prison are removed, there is little incentive for prisoners to behave, which makes the jobs of guards and officials much more difficult.

Correction Officer Charles Robinson stands at the edge of the gymnasium at Cybulski Correctional Institution. From his vantage point, he can see across the room.

In front of him, a handball smacks off a wall of the gym, creating a rhythmic cadence with the grunts of two inmates. Prisoners are shooting hoops on the other end of the expansive room. The metallic clang of weights echoes through the gym.

Some would look at this scene as an example of a weak prison system, full of fun for convicted felons. After many years as a guard, Robinson sees it differently.

"This breaks up a lot of the monotony of the day," he said. "And it relieves some of the stress."

Wardens and correction officials say that weight rooms, basketball hoops, televisions, radios and other pleasantries accomplish two very important tasks inside a prison: They are a powerful management tool, and they occupy prisoners' time.

However, much of the public is fed up with crime, and pictures of basketball hoops and fully stocked libraries in prisons only make them more disgusted. Politicians, in recent years, have tapped into that frustration and called for the elimination of such amenities. In Connecticut, changes have been made, but they have been tempered by the reality that recreation and education serve an important purpose.

It's rhetoric vs. reality in the get-tough-on-crime '90s.

"The people who are in charge of running prisons have a much more practical view of the importance of amenities than outsiders, especially politicians," said Timothy Flanagan, dean of the college of criminal justice at Sam Houston State University in Texas.

"There clearly is a problem with public perception of prison life."

Keeping inmates on track

Willie Kelly Keaton Jr. slides large weights onto a big metal bar. Each makes a hollow ring as the platter-sized weights slap together. Keaton lies on the bench and presses more than 300 pounds over his chest several times. When it gets difficult, he grimaces and pushes the weights up two more times.

He leaps up with pride.

When Keaton first entered prison, he was out of shape and addicted to drugs. In prison, he has found God and the weight room. He said his mind and body are fit for the outside world.

"I can bench-press 405 pounds," said Keaton, who now is in another state prison. "It gives me a lot of confidence to know that I can do that. And all the girls like a man with a healthy body." He laughs and flexes a muscle.

In the prison system, inmates are moved around among prisons and among security levels. So, Cybulski, in Somers, is the kind of place that many want to go to. It's still prison, but there are plenty of activities that help pass the days, or years, and sometimes help the prisoners straighten themselves out.

A variety of classes and programs available at Cybulski help prepare inmates for the free world—which is where a majority of them are heading within a year or two. There are bumper pool and pingpong tables in the dorms, a basketball court, a weight room, televisions and radios on almost every bunk, a library and other recreational and educational facilities.

Not all of Connecticut's prisons are like Cybulski. At Walker Special Management Unit in Suffield, for instance, recreation for higher-security inmates is a walk around in a cage. And at Northern Correctional Institution in Somers, the state's most secure prison, recreation consists of shuffling in circles around a concrete, open-air pen, in shackles.

Cybulski's inmates are usually charged with less-serious crimes and are fairly close to being released. The amenities they receive are linked to their attending counseling sessions, getting their high school diplomas and following the rules.

The prison's warden believes that recreation, special classes and other privileges help inmates stay on the right track.

"It keeps inmates busy and keeps them focused positive," said warden Sandra Sawicki. "It's a privilege to be here. They know that."

While the gymnasium hums with the sounds of "rec," on the other side of the institution, groups of men take a variety of classes.

Inmate George Gaston recently went through a major test in his job skills class—a mock interview. A teacher and the school principal peppered the would-be job candidate with pointed questions.

Why should we give you this job over other candidates?

"My focus would be on getting the job done," Gaston replied, choosing his words carefully.

Do you have a criminal background?

"Yes, I do, for possession of drugs," Gaston said. "It was an unfortunate experience. But it gave me the opportunity to graduate from community college."

Why won't you offend again? Gaston, who has since been sent to a halfway house and has a job, paused. "I believe incarceration did serve its job as a deterrent."

Club Med

In 1994, gubernatorial candidate John G. Rowland stood before blown-up pictures of basketball hoops and an electronic scoreboard at the yet-to-open York Correctional Institution, a women's prison in Niantic.

He blasted the prison as posh and compared it to a Club Med. It was, he said, a shining example of a state that is too soft on its criminals.

"The reality in Connecticut is that we're coddling our prisoners," he said and vowed to change it.

Such words tapped directly into voters' intolerance for crime and helped Rowland into the state's top job. Bashing prison amenities has become a common, and successful, political tactic. The argument resonates with many voters: Prison should not be a place people want to be.

"It can't be fun, like being outside of prison," said state Sen. John A. Kissel, R-Enfield. "That doesn't seem to mesh with my view of a tough correctional system."

Recreation, special classes and other privileges help inmates stay on the right track.

For years, Kissel has been trying to eliminate weightlifting in prisons. Bulked-up inmates are only more dangerous inside and outside the prisons.

"Essentially what you're doing is you're making criminals stronger," Kissel said.

Kissel has not been able to rid the prisons of weightlifting, but some changes have been made in state prison life. Despite Rowland's tough campaign words, the changes have been subtle and thoughtful.

"While (the prisons) haven't been turned into medieval dungeons, they certainly aren't as comfortable as they were in the past," said Nuala Forde, a spokeswoman for Rowland. "Prisons are not supposed to be comfortable."

Under state Correction Commissioner John J. Armstrong, some amenities have been eliminated or limited, and others have been linked more closely to a prisoner's behavior and classification within the system.

"We knew we had to change some ways that things in the Department of Correction were done," said Armstrong, a former guard who was one of Rowland's first major appointments.

Smoking has been snuffed out in all prisons, and inmates' access to phones and visits are tied to the security level of the prison they are in and their behavior. A contentious inmate may get no visits. Others may get "non-contact" visits, held through thick glass and over intercom phones, while lower-security, well-behaved inmates can sit at a table with their visitors.

Bashing prison amenities has become a common, and successful, political tactic.

Inmates still can purchase televisions at the commissary, but Armstrong said an inmate who misbehaves will have his or her TV packed up and sent home.

"And we'll charge them for the freight," he said.

The idea is to use such privileges as a management tool to control inmate behavior, while helping the prisoners prepare for the outside world.

"Privileges without accountability are not really privileges at all. They're entitlements," Armstrong said. "A system that has no distinction between good behavior and bad behavior is really a bear to manage."

Tent cities

On the outskirts of Phoenix, rows and rows of army tents are set up. It looks like a military compound, but the people inside are not soldiers—they're sentenced inmates under the comand of Sheriff Joe Arpaio.

Nationally, no one has galvanized the "get-tough-on-prisoners" movement like Arpaio.

As the head law enforcer in Arizona's Maricopa County, Arpaio enjoys a legendary reputation for being tough on criminals. He has erected the tent cities to house inmates sentenced to a year or less. There are no frills or niceties.

"Our men and women went to Saudi Arabia for Operation Desert Storm and lived in tents, and they didn't even commit a crime," Arpaio said. "Why would someone complain about putting convicted prisoners in tents?"

Twenty inmates bunk in each structure, and dogs with cameras strapped to their backs patrol the perimeter. The inmates have no basketball or weights, no coffee or cigarettes, no television. They eat lots of bologna. It saves money.

When Arpaio's inmates work in the community, they are chained together, and some wear striped prison uniforms.

"That's the way it should be," he said.

Arpaio has been re-elected sheriff—a powerful position in Arizona—and there has been talk of his running for governor. He also has written a book, *The Toughest Sheriff in America.*

"People are fed up with crime, and they want somebody to do something about it instead of talking about it," he said.

But not everyone feels that tent cities are the answer.

Prisoners who are simply warehoused like that will become more anti-social, some argue, and be more of a problem when they are released. Amenities give inmates something to do instead of causing trouble.

"Things like sports, that's just simple common sense. Most people in prison are of a young age and full of energy," said Jenni Gainsborough of the American Civil Liberties Union. "They are going to find some way of releasing it."

Without amenities to provide that release, she said, "prison becomes very difficult to manage, and it becomes very dangerous for the staff that works in there."

Nearly 400 inmates at the tent cities rioted in November [1996], setting fires and holding 11 guards hostage before getting a forum with Arpaio about the conditions at the prison.

Carrots and sticks

Inmates who have broken the rules at Cybulski find themselves at the desk of Correction Officer Scott Vanoudenhove, pleading their case and asking not to have their privileges revoked.

"Oh yeah, I've seen crying," Vanoudenhove said. "But usually they just whine and whine and whine."

Vanoudenhove can take away some or all of an inmate's privileges or even recommend that an inmate be sent to another, more restrictive, prison.

It's an example of what many prison officials already know—amenities are a great carrot.

"These programs become the carrots and sticks," said Flanagan, Sam Houston's dean of criminal justice. "You eliminate them, you eliminate the carrots and sticks."

Sam Houston State University surveyed more than 800 prison wardens, superintendents and commissioners in 1996 about the usefulness of amenities in prisons. The administrators overwhelmingly supported the presence of recreation, televisions and educational programs inside the prison walls.

More than 800 prison wardens, superintendents and commissioners . . . overwhelmingly supported the presence of recreation, televisions and educational programs inside the prison walls.

The majority of administrators surveyed endorsed the presence of weightlifting equipment, intramural sports, crafts and hobby programs and other activities in their institutions. Less than 25 percent felt televisions, VCRs, radios and musical instruments should be reduced or eliminated.

"Amenities provide incentives for inmates to stay out of trouble," Flanagan said. "We do need to consider what it's like to work in these institutions."

At Cybulski, one of the harshest punishments meted out by Vanoudenhove is CTQ, or confinement to quarters. An inmate given CTQ must stay in his bunk area, which is about the size of a walk-in closet. No napping is allowed. There's just lots of time to read and think. William Murcelo, 22, recently used the time to catch up on his Bible reading.

He had been on a work detail to Northern Correctional Institution—a nearby maximum-security prison—and was caught trying to smuggle employee cigarette butts back into Cybulski.

Murcelo, bored and remorseful, said he knew that if he slipped up again, he could be shipped to a higher-security prison and lose many of his privileges permanently. But he swore that wouldn't happen.

"This time, I'm gonna chill down," he said.

6

Convicted Felons Deserve the Right to Vote

Jamie Fellner and Marc Mauer

Jamie Fellner is an associate counsel for Human Rights Watch, an organization dedicated to protecting the human rights of people around the world. Marc Mauer is assistant director of the Sentencing Project, an independent source of criminal justice policy analysis, data, and program information for the public and policy makers. Both are co-authors of the report "Losing the Vote: The Impact of Felony Disenfranchisement Laws in the United States."

In forty-six states and the District of Columbia, convicted felons in prison cannot vote. In fourteen of those states, felons are barred from voting for life. Other states allow ex-offenders to vote, but the procedure to obtain such a privilege is all but impossible. Disenfranchisement affects African-Americans the most because a disproportionate number of them are incarcerated. Disenfranchisement laws cannot be justified under any circumstances because of the negative impact such laws have on the voting population. Changes need to be made in order to restore the vote to both prisoners and ex-offenders.

In forty-six states and the District of Columbia, criminal disenfranchisement laws deny the vote to all convicted adults in prison. Thirty-two states also disenfranchise felons on parole; twenty-nine disenfranchise those on probation. And, under laws that may be unique in the world, in fourteen states even ex-offenders who have fully served their sentences remain barred from voting for life.

An estimated 3.9 million U.S. citizens are disenfranchised, including over one million who have fully completed their sentences. That so many people are disenfranchised is an unintended consequence of harsh criminal justice policies that have increased the number of people sent to prison and the lengths of their sentences, despite a falling crime rate.

Reprinted, with permission, from "Nearly Four Million Americans Denied Vote Because of Felony Convictions," by Jamie Fellner and Marc Mauer, *Overcrowded Times*, October 1998.

The racial impact of disenfranchisement laws is particularly striking. Thirteen percent of African American men—1.4 million—are disenfranchised. This is more than one-third (36 percent) of the total disenfranchised population. In Alabama and Florida, almost one in three black men is disenfranchised. In eight other states, one in four black men is disenfranchised. If current trends continue, the rate could reach 40 percent in the states that disenfranchise ex-offenders.

Disenfranchisement laws in the U.S. are a vestige of medieval times when offenders were banished from the community and suffered civil death. Brought from Europe to the colonies, they gained new political salience at the end of the nineteenth century when disgruntled whites in a number of Southern states tailored them and other ostensibly race-neutral voting restrictions in an effort to exclude blacks from the vote.

Deprivation of the right to vote is not an inherent or necessary aspect of criminal punishment.

In the late twentieth century, the laws have no discernible legitimate purpose. Deprivation of the right to vote is not an inherent or necessary aspect of criminal punishment nor does it promote the reintegration of offenders into lawful society. Indeed, defenders of these laws have been hard pressed to justify them: they most frequently cite the patently inadequate goal of protecting against voter fraud or the anachronistic and untenable objective of preserving the "purity of the ballot box" by excluding voters lacking in virtue.

The extent of disenfranchisement in the United States is as troubling as the fact that the right to vote can be lost for relatively minor offenses. An offender who receives probation for a single sale of drugs can face a lifetime of disenfranchisement.

This article, drawing on a report recently released by The Sentencing Project and Human Rights Watch (Fellner and Mauer 1998), summarizes findings from the first fifty-state survey of the impact of U.S. criminal disenfranchisement laws. Among the key findings:

- An estimated 3.9 million Americans have currently or permanently lost the right to vote because of a felony conviction.
- 1.4 million disenfranchised persons are ex-offenders who have completed their criminal sentences. Another 1.4 million are on probation or parole.
- Thirteen percent of the black adult male population is disenfranchised, a rate seven times the national average. More than one-third (36 percent) of those disenfranchised are black men.
- Ten states disenfranchise more than one in five adult black men: in seven, one in four black men is *permanently* disenfranchised.
- Given current rates of incarceration, three in ten of the next generation of black men will be disenfranchised at some point in their lifetimes. In states with the most restrictive voting laws, 40 percent of black men are likely to be *permanently* disenfranchised.

Felony disenfranchisement

In the United States, conviction of a felony carries collateral "civil" consequences apart from penal sanctions such as fines or imprisonment. Offenders may lose the right to vote, to serve on a jury, or to hold public office, among other "civil disabilities" that may continue long after a criminal sentence has been served.

Maine, Massachusetts, Utah, and Vermont do not disenfranchise convicted felons. However, efforts are underway in Massachusetts and Utah to change that. In Massachusetts, state legislators have passed a constitutional amendment to strip prisoners of their voting rights; it must be voted on again in 1999. In Utah, voters in the November 1998 elections will consider a proposed constitutional amendment to bar felons from voting, but prisoners would regain the right to vote upon discharge from prison. [Both amendments were passed in favor of disenfranchisement.] The other forty-six states and the District of Columbia have disenfranchisement laws that deprive convicted offenders of the right to vote while in prison. In thirty-two states, convicted offenders may not vote while on parole, and twenty-nine of these states disenfranchise offenders on probation. State disenfranchisement laws and laws governing other civil disabilities are summarized in Office of U.S. Pardon Attorney (1996).

Most remarkably, in fourteen states, ex-offenders who have fully served their sentences nonetheless remain disenfranchised. Ten disenfranchise ex-felons for life: Alabama, Delaware, Florida, Iowa, Kentucky, Mississippi, Nevada, New Mexico, Virginia, and Wyoming. Arizona and Maryland permanently disenfranchise those convicted of a second felony. Tennessee and Washington disenfranchise permanently those convicted prior to 1986 and 1984, respectively. In addition, in Texas, a convicted felon's right to vote is not restored until two years after discharge from prison, probation, or parole.

State disenfranchisement laws have a dramatically disproportionate racial impact.

In theory, ex-offenders can regain the right to vote. In practice, this possibility is usually illusory. In eight states, a pardon or order from the governor is required; in two states, the ex-felons must obtain action by the parole or pardons board. Released ex-felons are not routinely informed about the steps necessary to regain the vote and often believe—incorrectly—that they can never vote again. Moreover, even if they seek to have the vote restored, few have the financial and political resources needed to succeed. In Virginia, for example, there are 200,000 ex-convicts, and only 404 had their vote restored in 1996 and 1997. In Mississippi, an ex-convict who wants to vote must either secure an executive order from the governor or get a state legislator to introduce a bill on his behalf, convince two-thirds of the legislators in each house to vote for it, and have it signed by the governor.

Most state disenfranchisement laws provide that conviction of any felony or crime that is punishable with imprisonment is a basis for losing the right to vote. The crime need not have any connection to electoral processes, nor need it be classified as notably serious. Shoplifting or possession of a modest amount of marijuana could suffice.

Department of Justice data indicates that an estimated one in twenty of today's children . . . will be disenfranchised.

Criminal disenfranchisement can follow conviction of either a state or federal felony. According to the U.S. Department of Justice, however, "not all states have paid consistent attention to the place of federal offenders in the state's scheme for loss and restoration of civil rights. While some state statutes expressly address federal offenses . . . , many do not. The disabilities imposed upon felons under state law generally are assumed to apply with the same force whether the conviction is a state or federal one" (Office of U.S. Pardon Attorney 1996, p. 2). In at least sixteen states, federal offenders cannot use the state procedure for restoring their civil rights. The only method provided by federal law for restoring voting rights to ex-offenders is a presidential pardon.

As a result of the considerable variation among the states, disenfranchisement laws form a national "crazy quilt." Within the federal structure of the U.S., it may be appropriate that each state determine voting qualifications for local and state offices. But state voting laws also govern eligibility to vote in federal elections. Exercise of the right to vote for national representatives is thus subject to the arbitrary accidents of geography. In Massachusetts, a convicted burglar may vote in national elections while he is in prison, but in Indiana he cannot. A person convicted of theft in New Jersey automatically regains the right to vote after release from prison, while in New Mexico such an offender is denied the vote for the rest of her life unless she can secure a pardon from the governor. In some states an offender who commits a felony and receives probation can vote, while in other states an offender guilty of the same crime who receives probation cannot.

Current impact

Using national conviction and corrections data, we estimate that 3.9 million Americans, including 1.4 million black men, cannot vote because of felony convictions. These national figures mask wide disparities among the states.

In addition, individual voting practices within the states may or may not conform to state law. This is a result both of inaccurate recordkeeping in some instances and misinformation in others. In states that disenfranchise ex-felons, election officials do not always have ready access to felony conviction data, and some ex-felons may vote. In other states where ex-felons are permitted to vote, released prisoners are not necessarily informed of this right and often incorrectly believe that they can never vote again.

The national rate of disenfranchisement, particularly for black men, is substantial. Not surprisingly, states that disenfranchise felons for life have far greater numbers of disenfranchised adults than other states.

- A total of 3.9 million adults, or 2.0 percent of the eligible voting population, is currently or *permanently* disenfranchised as a result of a felony conviction.
- Six states—Alabama, Florida, Mississippi, New Mexico, Virginia, and Wyoming—exclude more than 4 percent of their adult population from the vote.
- Florida and Texas each disenfranchise more than 600,000 people.
- Alabama, California, and Virginia each disenfranchise close to a quarter of a million persons.

Racial impact

State disenfranchisement laws have a dramatically disproportionate racial impact. Thirteen percent of all adult black men—1.4 million—are disenfranchised, representing one-third of the total disenfranchised population. That rate is seven times the national average. Election voting statistics offer an approximation of the political importance of black disenfranchisement: 1.4 million black men are disenfranchised compared with 4.6 million black men who voted in 1996.

The racial impact in certain individual states is extraordinary:

- In Alabama and Florida, 31 percent of all black men are permanently disenfranchised.
- In five other states—Iowa, Mississippi, New Mexico, Virginia, and Wyoming—one in four black men (24 to 28 percent) is *permanently* disenfranchised. In Washington state, one in four black men (24 percent) is currently or *permanently* disenfranchised.
- In Delaware, one in five black men (20 percent) is *permanently* disenfranchised.
- In Texas, one in five black men (20.8 percent) is currently disenfranchised.
- In four states—Minnesota, New Jersey, Rhode Island, and Wisconsin—16 to 18 percent of black men are currently disenfranchised.
- In nine states—Arizona, Connecticut, Georgia, Maryland, Missouri, Nebraska, Nevada, Oklahoma, and Tennessee—10 to 15 percent of black men are currently disenfranchised.

Incarceration policies

The number of people disenfranchised reflects to some extent the number of people involved in criminal activity. However, the proportion of the population that is disenfranchised has been exacerbated in recent years by the advent of such sentencing policies as mandatory minimum sentences, "three strikes" laws, and truth-in-sentencing laws. Although crime rates have been relatively stable or declining in the 1990s, these laws have increased the number of offenders sent to prison and the lengths of time they serve.

In California, for example, more than 40,000 offenders have been sentenced under the state's "three strikes" law as of June 1998. As a result of the law, 89 percent of these offenders had their sentences doubled, and 11 percent received sentences of twenty-five years to life. Only one in five were sentenced for crimes against persons; two-thirds were sentenced for a nonviolent drug or property crime. Seventy percent of the sentenced offenders were black or Hispanic.

The effects of changed sentencing policies are readily apparent from Department of Justice data. For example, persons arrested for burglary had a 53 percent greater likelihood of being sentenced to prison in 1992 than in 1980, while those arrested for larceny experienced a 100 percent increase. The most dramatic change can be seen for drug offenses, where arrestees were almost five times as likely to be sent to prison in 1992 as in 1980. In addition, since the number of drug arrests nearly doubled during this period, the impact was magnified further. Over this same twelve-year period, the rate of incarceration in prisons rose from 139 to 332 per 100,000 U.S. residents. Eighty-four percent of the increase in state prison admissions during this period was due to incarceration of nonviolent offenders.

The rate of incarceration has continued to soar. In 1997 the combined prison and jail rate reached 645 per 100,000 residents, the second-highest known rate of incarceration in the world (only Russia's is known to be higher). At year-end 1997 (the latest available figures), there were nearly 1.8 million U.S. residents incarcerated, two-thirds in state or federal prisons and the remainder in jails. At mid-year 1997, one in every 117 men and one in every 1,852 women were under the jurisdiction of state or federal correctional authorities. Fifty-three percent of state inmates were sentenced for nonviolent offenses (Bureau of Justice Statistics 1998).

If these incarceration rates remain unchanged, Department of Justice data indicate that an estimated one in twenty of today's children will serve time in a prison during his or her lifetime and will be disenfranchised for at least the period of incarceration (Bureau of Justice Statistics 1997). The total number of disenfranchised will be substantially greater because it will also include felons on probation in the twenty-nine states that disenfranchise those on probation.

Racially disproportionate incarceration rates

The strikingly disproportionate rate of disenfranchisement among black men reflects their disproportionate rate of incarceration. The rate of imprisonment for black men in 1996 was 8.5 times that for white men: black men were confined in prison at a rate of 3,098 per 100,000 compared to a white rate of 370. Even more strikingly, in the past ten years the black men's rate increased ten times more than the white men's increase (Bureau of Justice Statistics 1998).

If current rates of incarceration remain unchanged, 28.5 percent of black men will be confined in prison at least once during their lifetimes, a figure six times greater than for white men (Bureau of Justice Statistics 1997). As a result, nearly three in ten adult black men will be temporarily or permanently deprived of the right to vote. But the total numbers of disenfranchised will be greater because it will include those convicted of a felony but not receiving a prison sentence. In states that disenfranchise ex-felons, 40 percent of the next generation of black men is likely to lose the right to vote permanently.

We have not developed estimates of the number and racial composition of disenfranchised women. The rates for black women are also likely to be quite disproportionate, though on a smaller scale. This is a result both of increasing rates of criminal justice supervision of women, in general, and higher rates overall for black women, in particular. Although women represent 15 percent of all persons under correctional supervision, their numbers have been growing at faster rates than men's in recent years. Since black women are incarcerated at a rate eight times that for white women, the effect of these increases is magnified for them.

The increased rate of black imprisonment is a direct and foreseeable consequence of harsher sentencing policies, particularly for violent crimes, and of the national "war on drugs." Although the black proportion of arrestees for violent crimes has remained relatively stable over the past two decades, blacks nonetheless continue to constitute a disproportionately large percentage of those arrested for violent crimes (43 percent in 1996); their incarceration rate in part reflects the longer sentences imposed for those crimes. But drug control policies that have led to the arrest, prosecution, and imprisonment of tens of thousands of black Americans are the most dramatic change in factors contributing to their disproportionate rate of incarceration. Although drug use and selling cut across all racial, socioeconomic, and geographic lines, law enforcement strategies have targeted street-level drug dealers and users from low-income, predominantly minority, urban areas. As a result, the arrest rates per 100,000 for drug offenses are six times higher for blacks than for whites. Although the black proportion of all drug users is generally in the range of 13 to 15 percent, blacks constitute 36 percent of those arrested for drug possession. Under harsh drug sentencing policies, convictions for drug offenses have led to predictable skyrocketing in the number of blacks in prison. In 1985 there were 16,600 blacks in state prisons for drug offenses; by 1995 the number had reached 134,000. Between 1990 and 1996, 82 percent of the increase in the number of black federal inmates was due to drug offenses (Blumstein 1993; Tonry 1995).

Disenfranchisement cannot be justified

The practice of disenfranchising felons is a political anomaly in the United States. Voting is now a basic right possessed by all mentally competent adults except those convicted of felonies.

Depriving citizens of a political right should only be undertaken for compelling reasons and only to the extent necessary to further those interests. But felony disenfranchisement laws in the United States are not necessary to further any substantial state interests. The fact that disenfranchisement laws have long historical roots is, of course, an inadequate justification for retaining them: as standards of decency and political rights evolve, societies continually reject practices that were formerly acceptable.

Denying the vote to ex-offenders

There is little good to be gained from disenfranchising ex-felons who have served their time. As Supreme Court Justice Thurgood Marshall stated: "It is doubtful . . . whether the state can demonstrate either a compelling or rational policy interest in denying former felons the right to vote. [Ex-offenders] have fully paid their debt to society. They are as much affected by the actions of government as any other citizen, and have as much of a right to participate in governmental decision-making. Furthermore, the denial of a right to vote to such persons is hindrance to the efforts of society to rehabilitate former felons and convert them into law-abiding and productive citizens." *Richardson v. Ramirez,* 418 U.S. at 78 (1974).

Supporters of disenfranchisement have been hard pressed to identify the state interests furthered by denying the vote to ex-offenders. The most frequently cited interests are these: (1) protection against voter fraud or other election offenses; (2) prevention of harmful changes to the law; and (3) protection of the "purity" of the ballot box. But there are severe problems with each one of these putative interests.

Protection against voter fraud is clearly an insufficient rationale for statutes that are triggered by crimes having nothing to do with elections, where laws criminalizing voter fraud exist, and where there is no evidence that ex-felons are more likely than anyone else to commit voter fraud.

The second alleged state interest is equally inadequate. There is no reason to believe that all or even most ex-offenders would vote to weaken the content or administration of criminal laws. Conditioning the right to vote on the content of the vote contradicts the very principle of universal suffrage.

Some might argue that disenfranchisement of ex-felons is simply another penalty the state chooses to impose in addition to incarceration, although there is little historical basis for this view. It is questionable whether a state may punish offenders by depriving them of any right it chooses. Would a state be able to punish felons by forever denying them the right to go to court or to petition the government? But even if one assumes that deprivation of the right to vote is a legitimate punishment, then such punishment must conform to the fundamental principles governing criminal sanctions. It should, for example, be imposed by a judge following trial, and it should be proportionate to the offense. Yet none of the states requires that disenfranchisement be imposed by a judge as part of a criminal sentence. And disenfranchisement laws operate without regard to the seriousness of the crime or the severity of the sentence. A person convicted of a single relatively minor crime who never serves any prison time can be turned into a political "outcast" for life. Decades after the crime was committed and the sentence served, regardless of however exemplary the ex-offender's subsequent life may have been, he or she is still denied the ability to exercise the most basic constitutive act of citizenship in a democracy: the right to vote.

Denying the vote to ex-offenders accomplishes little of value. Indeed, it may do more harm than good. Disenfranchisement contradicts the promise of rehabilitation. As the National Advisory Commission on Criminal Justice Standards and Goals (1973) observed, "If correction is to reintegrate an offender into free society, the offender must retain all attributes of citizenship . . . ."

Representative John Conyers, Jr., a member of Congress who has unsuccessfully championed federal legislation that would restore the franchise to ex-felons, has cogently summarized his reasons for permitting them to vote: "If we want former felons to become good citizens, we must give them rights as well as responsibilities, and there is no greater responsibility than voting."

Denying the vote to incarcerated citizens

The widespread and historical practice in the United States of denying the vote to convicted citizens while they are in prison—or even while on probation or parole—has received little scrutiny. To many people the practice may seem an inevitable concomitant of incarceration or a legitimate additional punishment for a crime. It is neither.

A sentence of imprisonment does not strip a person of all his or her rights. One loses the right to liberty—which is why incarceration is such a severe punishment—but retains all other rights subject only to those reasonable restrictions that promote the safe, orderly, and secure functioning of prisons. Common sense indicates that the unfettered exercise in prison of the rights of freedom of movement and association would jeopardize the ability of prison authorities to maintain control. There is no plausible argument, however, that permitting inmates to vote, e.g., by absentee ballot, would interfere with prison operations or administration.

A sentence of imprisonment does not strip a person of all his or her rights.

Viewed as additional punishment, the disenfranchisement of incarcerated felons suffers the same problems as the disenfranchisement of ex-felons, e.g., lack of proportionality and absence of participation by a judge. In addition, given that incarcerated offenders are suffering all the losses and hardships that necessarily attend life behind bars, a state's interest in inflicting even more punishment can scarcely be weighty enough to justify deprivation of another fundamental right.

Disenfranchisement in other countries

The United States may have the world's most restrictive criminal disenfranchisement laws. We know of no other democracy besides the United States in which convicted offenders who have served their sentences are nonetheless disenfranchised for life. A few countries restrict the vote for a short period after conclusion of the prison term: Finland and New Zealand, for example, restrict the vote for several years after completion of sentence, but only in the case of persons convicted of buying or selling votes or of corrupt practices. Some countries condition disenfranchisement of prisoners on the seriousness of the crime or the length of their sentence. Others, e.g., Germany and France, permit disenfranchisement only when it is imposed by a court order.

Many countries permit persons in prison to vote. According to research by Penal Reform International, prisoners may vote in countries as diverse as the Czech Republic, Denmark, France, Israel, Japan, Kenya, Netherlands, Norway, Peru, Poland, Romania, Sweden, and Zimbabwe. In Germany, the law obliges prison authorities to encourage prisoners to assert their voting rights and to facilitate voting procedures. The only prisoners who may not vote are those convicted of electoral crimes or crimes (e.g., treason) that undermine the "democratic order," and whose court-imposed sentence expressly includes disenfranchisement.

Implementing change

Felony voting restrictions in the U.S. are political anachronisms reflecting values incompatible with modern democratic principles. At the edge of the millennium these laws have no purpose. To the contrary, they arbitrarily deny convicted offenders the ability to vote regardless of the nature of their crimes or the severity of their sentences, they create political "outcasts" from taxpaying, law-abiding citizens who are ex-offenders, they distort the country's electoral process, and they diminish the black vote, countering decades of voting rights gains.

The impact of felony disenfranchisement laws has been exacerbated in the past quarter century as more offenders are convicted of felonies, more convicted felons are sent to prison, and prison sentences have grown longer. These trends reflect the adoption of public policies that emphasize incarceration and punishment as the principal means of crime control. While debate continues about the wisdom and efficacy of such policies, it is clear that they have had many unintended consequences—one of which is the significant increase in the disenfranchised population.

Given the major impact of felony disenfranchisement laws on the voting population, and in particular their strikingly disproportionate impact on black Americans, policy makers should consider alternative policies that will better protect voting rights without injury to legitimate state criminal justice interests. We believe the best course of action would be to remove conviction-based restrictions on voting rights. At the federal level, Congress should enact legislation to restore voting rights in federal elections to citizens convicted of a felony, so that the ability to vote in federal elections is not subject to varying state laws. State legislatures should also eliminate state laws that curtail the franchise for persons with felony convictions within their states.

To the extent that legislators believe that incarcerated offenders should be excluded from the franchise, any legislation in this area should identify the important state interests served by such disenfranchisement; specify the crimes for which disenfranchisement is a reasonable and proportionate response; and require that imprisoned offenders be excluded from voting only if loss of the vote is imposed by a judge as part of a criminal sentence. Such legislation should also specify that restoration of the right to vote following release from prison is automatic and immediate.

Note

"Losing the Vote: The Impact of Felony Disenfranchisement Laws in the United States," the report on which this article is based, may be obtained from The Sentencing Project, 918 F Street N.W., Suite 501, Washington, D.C. 20004 (202) 628-0871; www.sentencingproject.org or Human Rights Watch, 350 Fifth Avenue, 34th Floor, New York, NY 10018 (212) 290-4700; www.hrw.org.

References

Blumstein, Alfred. 1993. "Racial Disproportionality of U.S. Prison Populations Revisited." *University of Colorado Law Review* 64:743–60.

Bureau of Justice Statistics. 1997. *Lifetime Likelihood of Going to State or Federal Prison*. Special Report NCJ-160092. Washington, D.C.: U.S. Department of Justice, Office of Justice Programs.

————. 1998. *Prisoners in 1997*. BJS Bulletin NCJ 170014. Washington, D.C.: U.S. Department of Justice, Office of Justice Programs.

National Advisory Commission on Criminal Justice Standards and Goals. 1973. *Task Force Report: Corrections*. Washington, D.C.: U.S. Government Printing Office.

Office of U.S. Pardon Attorney. 1996. *Civil Disabilities of Convicted Felons: A State-by-State Survey*. Washington, D.C.: U.S. Department of Justice.

Tonry, Michael. 1995. *Malign Neglect—Race, Crime, and Punishment in America*. New York: Oxford University Press.

7

Supermax Prisons Are Cruel and Inhumane

Spencer P.M. Harrington

Spencer P.M. Harrington is a freelance writer. He attended the John Jay College of Criminal Justice in New York and wrote this article with the support of a grant from the Dick Goldensohn Fund, which promotes investigative journalism.

Many prisons have created supermax units that include long-term solitary confinement and harsh conditions to control problem prisoners. Research has shown, however, that such confinement can cause psychosis in a sane prisoner, and greatly exacerbate problems in already mentally ill prisoners. Some prisoners are being released into society straight from these "supermax" prisons, and this poses a threat to public safety.

A steel door separates the Department Disciplinary Unit from the rest of the prison of Walpole, Massachusetts. Inmates confined in the DDU are considered management problems by staff. It is a prison within a prison: convicts housed here have no contact with each other or with other inmates at Walpole. They spend all of their waking hours alone in 8-by-10-foot cells, each with a narrow window in the back wall permitting minimal sunlight. They eat alone, are denied access to work or educational programs, and are entitled to five hours a week of solitary recreation in an empty 6-by-30-foot outdoor exercise cage surrounded by a chain-link fence. When the weather is bad, there is no recreation time at all. They can have no more than four books in their cells. People can be sentenced here for a maximum of 10 years but can spend longer than that if they disobey the rules. Serious infractions lead to disciplinary isolation, where they are permitted no phone calls, no visitors, no access to radio or television, no legal materials, no books, and, until recently, no exercise. It is possible to serve consecutive sentences in isolation, sometimes for a year or more.

Slowly, and with few people outside of corrections noticing, America's most secure prisons are locking down "problem" inmates 23 hours a day behind solid steel doors.

Reprinted from "Caging the Crazy: 'Supermax' Confinement Under Attack," by Spencer P.M. Harrington, *The Humanist*, January/February 1997, by permission of the author.

Whether they are called supermax or control units, punitive or administrative segregation areas, the conditions of confinement are usually the same. Inmates are housed in solitary. They eat and exercise alone. They are never allowed contact visits and are permitted few, if any, in-cell educational or vocational programs. Thirty-six states have embraced the idea of lockdown for their "problem" inmates; some have built spanking-new high-tech supermax prisons, while others have added high-security units like the DDU to existing facilities. In the newer prisons, most of the traditional jobs performed by staff—such as opening cell doors, listening to complaints, and surveillance—are now totally automated. With prison gangs now considered to be the greatest threat to institutional safety, correctional administrators have not hesitated to fill these supermax units with suspected members, even if they have committed no infractions. Some mental-health researchers say that mentally ill inmates are disproportionately represented in supermaxes, since they are often unable to control their disruptive behavior. Inmates are doing years in lockdown and then being released from supermaxes directly onto the streets with no pre-release programming.

Imagine taking a dog that has bitten someone, and kicking and beating and abusing it in a cage for a year.

In Massachusetts, for example, as of September 1995, 39 inmates had been released from the DDU without any pre-release counseling, according to Massachusetts Department of Corrections officials. "Imagine taking a dog that has bitten someone, and kicking and beating and abusing it in a cage for a year," says Stuart Grassian, a Boston psychiatrist who examined 32 DDU inmates for a suit pending against the Massachusetts Department of Corrections. "Then you take that cage and you put it in the middle of a city, you open it, and you hightail it out of there. That's what you're doing to these people. . . . This is not a service for public safety." He describes inmates who have spent long periods in supermax units as being high-strung, irritable, anti-social, potentially violent, sometimes mentally ill, and definitely at risk of recidivating. "I would not want to be the neighbors of the individuals that I knew and saw leave the DDU," says Robert Dellelo, 54, who is now serving a five-year DDU sentence for an escape attempt. "I have not only seen inmates who were aggressive and hostile but actually psychotic released onto the streets." Robert Verdeyen of the American Correctional Association acknowledges that it is "a pretty scary thought" to consider that supermax prisoners can be released directly into the community. But he adds, "If people serve every bit of time they're supposed to do, there's nothing anyone can do. . . . They're just released. They've paid their debt to society."

Attempts at reform

The courts have proved the sole avenue for penal reform. The Massachusetts litigation alleges cruel and unusual punishment in the DDU and is part of a larger trend of suits challenging supermax confinement on mental-health grounds. Historically, the judiciary has allowed great discretion to prison administrators in designing and operating correctional programs of their choosing. The courts have also never ruled that solitary confinement was so damaging to inmates' psyches that it constituted a violation of the Eighth Amendment ban on cruel and unusual punishment. Nevertheless, in *Madrid v. Gomez*, a well-publicized suit challenging conditions at northern California's Pelican Bay State Prison, a U.S. district court judge ruled that confinement in lockdown units was harmful to certain inmates, notably those with mental illnesses or those at risk of developing them.

In 1996, lawyers for mentally ill inmates confined in New Jersey prisons filed a class-action suit charging that the state Department of Corrections failed to provide them with adequate psychiatric care. The suit claims that the corrections department's own records show that a substantial proportion of inmates admitted to the state psychiatric hospital came from supermax units. Meanwhile, other supermaxes are coming under increasing scrutiny. A Colorado prisoners' rights group issued a report [in 1997] on the Colorado State Penitentiary, a Canon City supermax, noting that a quarter of the inmates housed there are on some form of anti-psychotic medication; they are also never allowed outdoors under any circumstances. The group also asked for a Department of Justice investigation.

Also in 1996, a Department of Justice inspection of the Maryland Correctional Adjustment Center, a Baltimore supermax, noted potential constitutional violations. The report pointed out that inmates were subjected to "extreme social isolation" and were kept alone in their cells 24 hours a day, except for a brief period (less than an hour) every two to three days when they were permitted to shower and walk around an indoor area. The Department of Justice noted that this isolation was "the mental equivalent of putting an asthmatic in a place with little air to breathe."

History of the penitentiary

The modern American penitentiary was born in the 1820s and 1830s and imbued with a moral dogma that still confuses our thinking about the role of prisons in our society.

At this time, there were two models of incarceration: the Auburn system, which emphasized punishment and deterrence, and the Pennsylvania system, which sought moral reformation. While the Auburn system was eventually adopted by most states, the Pennsylvania model was more popular in Europe, and its rehabilitative goal has, from time to time, exerted considerable influence over domestic prison policy. Americans send their criminals to prison as punishment, showing that most want them to be rehabilitated while locked up. Parole boards still look for evidence of reform and penitence, though many who study criminal justice acknowledge that our prisons are coercive warehouses that are incompatible with rehabilitation. Prison and punishment are dirty words in American "corrections," as the field is euphemistically known. Inmates who break prison rules are not punished but earn different "security classifications." Then they are sent to horrifying places where the corrections lingo fools no one. They are being punished.

Auburn Prison in New York was built between 1816 and 1821. Upon completion, its board of inspectors stated that its purpose was to confine felons "in solitary cells and dungeons," their reformation being of "minor consideration." Convicts in Auburn's northern wing were confined in solitary without any opportunity to work or leave their cells. Eighteen months after this experiment began, Auburn's administrators realized they had been overzealous. On an official visit to the prison, New York Governor Joseph C. Yates witnessed one man spring from his cell the moment the door was opened and hurl himself from the gallery to the pavement. Another prisoner was witnessed beating his head against the wall of his cell until he had put one of his eyes out. After this false start, Auburn's penal philosophy changed. Convicts were confined alone in their cells at night but worked together in silence during the day. Frequent beatings were administered to make inmates work and to enforce the silence rule. This system of congregate labor had the great advantage of making Auburn inexpensive to operate, and the prison became the prototype for institutions across the country.

Yates witnessed one man spring from his cell the moment the door was opened and hurl himself from the gallery to the pavement.

The Pennsylvania system established in Eastern State Penitentiary in Philadelphia was more expensive to operate but had loftier goals. The Quakers who ran the prison believed that convicts had a tendency to corrupt one another and that solitary confinement with the Bible (the only book allowed) would serve a rehabilitative purpose. Work was also considered beneficial, and convicts were permitted to pursue trades in their cells.

When it opened in 1829, Eastern State was the largest and most expensive public-works project of its time, costing $653,125. The prison, which still stands, was designed by English architect John Haviland to resemble a medieval castle. It has seven radial cellhouses connected to a central rotunda which served as an observatory and guardhouse. Like the Auburn system, inmates were to have no communication with fellow prisoners. But unlike Auburn, this mandate was enforced not with the whip but by solitary confinement. Eastern State enforced this solitude with a variety of innovations. No one was needed to provide wood for in-cell stoves because Haviland installed central heating. Flush toilets insured that inmates would not wander the halls and commingle while on their way to a communal privy. Inmates were allowed outdoors once a day in a walled-off area attached to each cell. Outdoor time was scheduled so as to avoid inmates in adjacent cells from communicating over their walled dog-runs. All 583 convicts ate in their cells. The modern history of the supermax began on Saturday, October 22, 1983, when Thomas Silverstein, an inmate at the federal maximum-security penitentiary in Marion, Illinois, stabbed a corrections officer 40 times, precipitating a total lockdown of the prison. The guard was one of two corrections officers to die that day in separate incidents. The Federal Bureau of Prisons reacted by converting Marion into a disciplinary institution to confine inmates considered escape risks or especially dangerous. The Bureau of Prisons established the now-familiar routine for inmates in segregation: solitary confinement, 23-hour lockdown, in-cell meals. Isolating convicts became a trend as state penitentiaries soon began to "Marionize." Marion was the model for programs adopted in prisons at McAlester, Oklahoma, in 1985, at Pelican Bay, California, in 1989, at Southport, New York, in 1991, and at Walpole, Massachusetts, in 1992.

Prison administrators like supermaxes for a variety of reasons. First, they believe that, by isolating difficult inmates in one secure facility, they will decrease disruptive behavior at their other prisons. California, Colorado, and New York prison officials credit the introduction of supermaxes with a reduction in violent incidents systemwide. Second, they believe supermaxes provide a safe environment for staff, because inmates are nearly always behind bars. "If these conditions are harsh, you have to remember that we're talking about some very violent people who have typically either killed other inmates or staff after they've been in prison," says Verdeyen. "We're talking about very, very violent people." Third, prison administrators think supermaxes are deterrents; they offer prison officials an option of last resort for disruptive convicts. Fourth, supermaxes are convenient places to stash "revolutionary" inmates, gang leaders, or those who administrators think might stir up trouble. And finally, because supermaxes are so automated and provide so few programs to inmates, their operation is theoretically cost-efficient.

Psychological effects of supermax confinement

But some mental-health researchers worry that supermax confinement is not in the best interests of society.

Boston psychiatrist Stuart Grassian and psychology professor Craig Haney of the University of California at Santa Cruz have emerged as the most articulate critics of "Marionization," and it was their testimony that helped sway the court in the *Madrid v. Gomez* suit. John Rheinstein, the Massachusetts Civil Liberties Union lawyer who filed suit over DDU conditions in his state, says that, if the case ever goes to trial, it will "rise or fall with Grassian's testimony." Grassian is a clinical instructor in psychiatry at Harvard Medical School and has published and lectured on the psychiatric effects of solitary confinement. Haney, in addition to his psychology professorship, is a lawyer and the director of the university's legal studies program. Both men have testified numerous times in prison litigation.

Haney describes the trend toward supermaxes as a major shift in the focus of American corrections, perhaps the most significant change since the abandonment of rehabilitation in the mid-1970s. He says this trend toward isolation units has occurred with very little public awareness. The marriage of technology with modern prison architecture has minimized staff-inmate contact in these prisons, despite studies showing that such contact can diffuse hostility and violence. Guards working at supermaxes "never see inmates in any even semi-normal context," Haney says. "They're always in their cells, under surveillance, in chains, being escorted, never interacting with anyone in anything that approximates a human context. I think that has an eroding effect over time in terms of their ability to understand these guys as people." As a result, staff view the inmates as monsters and treat them as such.

According to Haney, supermaxes represent another change from traditional punitive confinement in that inmates are serving their entire sentences in isolation. Whereas in the past inmates were sent to the "hole" (punitive isolation) for weeks or even months as punishment, the idea was always to reintegrate them back into prison society. "Now the notion is that these guys are just going to be (in isolation) forever," he says. "They're going to be there until they parole or die." Haney explains that in the past the hole was a small part of a larger prison that typically included some activities or resources. Prisoners serving time in the hole might be able to avail themselves of at least some diversion, from a correspondence course to a book cart. But now, with entire prisons and special units devoted solely to punitive confinement, it's more difficult for inmates in isolation to access any of the prison's resources, mostly because they don't exist.

These places are about as dysfunctional as you can imagine.

The most insidious effect of isolation is that it can destroy an inmate's ties to society. According to Haney, "You can go up to Pelican Bay on any given day, and there are 1,500 guys in the [Security Housing Unit], and I'll bet you $100 that, on the day you go, there will not be a single visitor in the visiting room. It's 1,500 miles from southern California and, when you get there, your inmate is brought out in chains and put into a little booth. The only thing you can do is talk to him over a telephone and look through a great big, thick glass partition. You can't even touch their hand. And what happens is that these guys paradoxically retreat further and further into themselves, and so they discourage even the visitors who are willing to endure all of that, because they become very uncomfortable around people." Haney says that marriages dissolve and relationships with children wither. "The people with the worst prospects for successfully adjusting to the free world once they're released from prison are those who come out with nobody to rely on," he says. "These places are about as dysfunctional as you can imagine for providing them with the resources to make that transition work."

Though supermax confinement has existed for more than 10 years, there have been no follow-up studies at these institutions tracking ex-convicts who were confined for lengthy periods in isolation. "It would seem to me," Haney says, "that, in a rationally organized society, before we committed hundreds of millions of dollars [to prison construction], we'd want to do some careful followup of the few supermaxes that have existed for quite a while." Both Haney and Grassian have only anecdotal evidence of the long-term ill effects of supermax confinement, and the little information they have about its effects is not comforting. Both have been contacted by about a half-dozen inmates who were released from the Pelican Bay SHU only to commit murder or other serious felonies.

"I'm not going to argue that anybody and everybody who goes into a control unit like the SHU comes out a raving maniac," says Haney. "But

I would say that I don't know of instances of people being benefited by it. I think it varies as to the amount of harm inflicted. Some people come out and they manage to adjust reasonably well afterward, but they have the resources—mental and otherwise—to rebound from the experience. But even among people who were otherwise healthy, some of them never recover. I've looked at files of people who had no preexisting psychological problems who went to Pelican Bay, began to deteriorate, and some of them are still in psychiatric crisis."

Grassian says he has identified a psychiatric syndrome associated with the sensory deprivation of solitary confinement. This syndrome, he says, includes a constellation of symptoms rarely, if ever, found outside conditions of social isolation, including hyperresponsivity to external stimuli (that is, the inability to tolerate certain smells and sounds); perceptual disturbances; difficulties with thinking, concentration, and memory; severe anxiety and agitation; and, in the most severe cases, onset of a confusional psychosis with severe agitation and paranoia. Grassian contends that this syndrome appears to be a form of delirium and meets diagnostic criteria for that syndrome. People with a history of cognitive impairment, seizure disorder, or attention-deficit hyperactivity are especially prone to this delirium in atmospheres of restricted environmental stimulation. According to Grassian, the greater the degree of social and sensory deprivation, the greater the chance someone will develop this syndrome. Similarly, the greater the amount of time spent in conditions of sensory deprivation, the greater the risk of the illness.

Grassian first saw symptoms of this delirium while examining inmates confined in solitary at Walpole during a 1979 lawsuit challenging conditions at the prison. "I didn't know what I was observing," he recalls. When he examined psychiatric literature on sensory deprivation, however, he found striking parallels. Grassian's research led him to the rare books room at the Harvard Medical School Library, where he found a 1912 summary of 50 years of psychiatric research on solitary confinement in German prisons. By the end of the nineteenth century, 37 articles in German medical journals had documented psychotic disturbances among inmates in the more than 40 prisons modeled after Philadelphia's Eastern State Penitentiary. In this summary, solitary confinement was identified as an important factor in the origin of these mental illnesses. The list was exhaustive. "These clinicians 100 and 150 years ago were speaking to me," says Grassian. "They were describing exactly the same thing that I had just seen. It was one of the most dramatic intellectual moments of my life."

A second opinion

Not all researchers agree with Grassian's warnings about the risks associated with sensory deprivation in solitary confinement. Some social scientists, especially psychologists, say that his research has been compromised by his involvement as an expert witness for inmate plaintiffs in class-action suits. Peter Suedfeld, a University of British Columbia professor of psychology who has conducted research on solitary confinement, says that there are "many, many convicts, political prisoners, and prisoners of war who have been held in solitary for several years and who came out of it without major mental breakdowns, and any psychiatrist or lawyer who implies that solitary confinement necessarily results in psychiatric breakdown is either ignorant or lying." Suedfeld says that conditions of isolation would have to be "very severe and quite prolonged—complete darkness, complete silence, complete isolation"—in order to induce mental illness in previously healthy inmates. He notes that few Vietnam prisoners of war and prisoners of the Gestapo went crazy, and both were tortured and held under these conditions. He feels that psychologists and psychiatrists who get involved in class-action suits "are essentially working against the prison system, and they don't have any particular interest in doing rigorous research. What they want to do is what Grassian is doing—intervene on behalf of inmates they think are being mistreated. And they don't want to do research that might show that they're wrong."

The one thing Suedfeld and Grassian agree on is that mentally ill offenders have no place in solitary confinement.

Exacerbating mental illness

There is little question that solitary confinement makes the psychotic even more psychotic. Grassian, however, thinks that correctional administrators are singling out the wrong inmates for punishment. "People generally have this notion that these are bad guys who do bad things and that, if you punish them, they won't do bad things," he explains. "But you're assuming that the inmate makes a rational calculation of means and ends, of actions and consequences. The kinds of people who are cold-blooded calculators aren't generally the kind of people who end up in solitary confinement. They usually end up in places where you can make big pots of pasta in minimum-security institutions. They're clever enough to know when it isn't worth breaking a rule." The people who end up in supermaxes, he says, are those who are "impulse-ridden, whose internal lives are chaotic, whose ability to calculate means and ends is very, very limited, or whose capacity to control their behavior in response to such a calculation is very, very limited." As a result, the more a mentally ill offender is punished, the more out of control he or she becomes. The more stringent the condition of confinement, Grassian adds, the greater the percentage of mentally ill inmates.

Academic research appears to bear this out. A 1991 study of isolation units in two maximum-security prisons in Quebec found that nearly a third of the inmates confined in long-term segregation had a severe mental illness. They were three times more likely to be schizophrenic than the general prison population, and 25 times more likely than nonincarcerated males. Nearly a quarter had attempted suicide.

David Lovell, a research assistant at the University of Washington's Department of Psychosocial and Community Health, is conducting a study of inmates referred to a special mental-health unit at the McNeil Island Correctional Center in Washington state. "Based on our sample," he says, "there appears to be a minority of mentally ill offenders who have had extremely disruptive prison careers and who have spent a lot of time in disciplinary settings, including segregation and intensive management units." He adds that the McNeil Island study corroborates other research indicating that the mentally ill get in trouble in disproportionate numbers and end up spending more time in lockdown. An earlier study by

Lovell and University of Washington colleague Ron Jemelka showed that, while offenders with serious mental illness constituted 18.7 percent of Washington state's prison population, they accounted for 41 percent of the infractions.

Mental-health researchers estimate that between 10 and 15 percent of the nation's one million prisoners have severe mental illnesses. Only those found not guilty by reason of insanity are housed in psychiatric hospitals—a standard that, according to David Lovell, is "pretty hard to meet in court, even for someone who is quite looney." So those not legally insane but still mentally ill often find themselves being shuttled between prisons and psychiatric hospitals—two institutions with profoundly different missions. Convicts will typically become ill behind bars, then be bused to a psychiatric hospital, where they will remain until they are stabilized. They are then bused back to prison, where they often become sick again.

While prisons are required to provide mental-health services, the recent explosion in the prison population has meant that there are fewer resources available for careful attention to the needs of the mentally ill. Haney says that there are just "too few mental-health personnel to do the kind of screening and monitoring that ought to be done throughout the system generally and during the disciplinary process in particular." As a result, he says, "quite a high percentage of people who are acting out because of their mental disorder are undetected, untreated, unmonitored, and end up in segregation units."

While both Haney and Grassian advocate confining mentally ill offenders in hospitals or, at least, in prisons with specially designed mental health units, both recognize that this is not about to happen soon. All available criminal-justice resources have been used for prison construction, and psychiatric hospitals that confine garden-variety mentally ill offenders are a thing of the past. Most are not secure enough and provide only short-term treatment.

There is little question that solitary confinement makes the psychotic even more psychotic.

Howard Zonana, medical director of the American Academy of Psychiatry and Law, says that confining mentally ill offenders in a secure psychiatric hospital would most likely be more expensive than traditional imprisonment. He also doubts that the mental-health community would want to take on the burden of incarceration. "If you transfer everyone to mental hospitals," he says, "the public expectation is that, if anyone ever gets released, they should be permanently cured. There's a zero-degree tolerance for any mentally ill person getting out and committing crimes. Whereas most people—while they don't like it—don't find it surprising that many people released from prison are rearrested. Wardens don't lose sleep over whether an inmate is going to get out and do something illegal again, whereas mental hospitals go crazy over that kind of stuff. They are held responsible."

Finally, there's a lack of political will to build secure mental hospitals. According to Haney, "You don't get a lot of support in the legislature by getting up and saying, 'We've got a lot of mentally ill prisoners and we've got to do something humane to deal with this problem.' The whole slant of political rhetoric over the past 15 to 20 years has been 'Kick 'em in the ass. Be as nasty as you can be.' If I were a legislator, I think it would be kind of hard to put it in a way that wouldn't cost me votes."

The prognosis for the future of inmate suits challenging supermax confinement on mental-health grounds is uncertain.

A responsibility to society

The Supreme Court has recently interpreted the Eighth Amendment prohibition of cruel and unusual punishment in a narrow manner. Plaintiffs must now prove the "deliberate indifference" of defendants. Such "state of mind" standards are notoriously difficult to prove. Inmates must show not only that their confinement constituted cruel and unusual punishment but that the prison staff meant for it to be so.

Making matters more difficult for inmate advocates, the Prison Litigation Reform Act, passed by President Clinton in April 1996, does not allow prisoners to sue for damages for psychological harm in federal courts unless there is a prior showing of physical harm. "This seems to say that psychological torture is okay in US prisons," says Jenni Gainsborough, public policy coordinator for the American Civil Liberties Union's National Prison Project. "As long as you don't leave any scars, you can get away with anything." Gainsborough notes that the law has not yet been subject to a court challenge because it is still so new. [The Prison Litigation Reform Act (PLRA) has been challenged numerous times since it was passed but it has not yet been overturned.]

> *Correctional administrators do have a responsibility . . . to make sure that convicts leave prison no worse than when they entered.*

The concentration of inmates who present management problems in one secure prison is not necessarily an unsound penological concept. But the idea becomes problematic when inmates are housed there for indefinite periods and are written off as monstrous incorrigibles deserving of none of the small pleasures—like natural light—that prison life can offer. Pelican Bay's SHU and Walpole's DDU wouldn't exist if correctional administrators thought that the loss of liberty associated with being in lockdown 23 hours a day were punishment enough. "This way of treating inmates," says Grassian, "is to punish them if they misbehave, and if they misbehave in that punishment setting, punish them more severely. So what you have to do is artfully keep finding worse and worse methods of punishing them. So this creates more and more elaborate systems of solitary confinement and longer and longer sentences there under very harsh conditions."

There's no question that more thorough studies of supermax confinement should be undertaken to determine whether the millions of dollars it takes to build these facilities is well spent. Prison disciplinary procedures that lead to supermax confinement also need to be reviewed. All too often, these disciplinary measures presuppose a rational, calculating convict who will be deterred from misbehavior by harsh conditions of confinement. Sadly, however, supermaxes imprison a large share of impulsive, chaotic, mentally ill people who are oblivious to a rational calculus of punishment and rewards. The more they are punished, the more out of control they become.

Since the vast majority of offenders will be back on the streets at one time or another, correctional administrators do have a responsibility to society, and that is to make sure that convicts leave prison no worse than when they entered.

8

Electronic Weapons Should Not Be Used to Control Prisoners

William F. Schulz

William F. Schulz writes for the New York Review of Books, *an intellectual magazine that focuses on topics ranging from politics and culture to literature.*

Shock weapons such as stun belts and shields have become more commonly used by prison officials in recent years. Labeled "crime control" devices, these weapons present several dangers. Prison officials are extremely apt to misuse the devices, and the weapons themselves may be dangerous, since there is no proof that shocks do not have long term medical effects. Finally, the United States has no way of guaranteeing that the shock weapons they export to other countries will not be used for torture.

During a break in his trial on charges of assault, Edward Valdez walked out of the San Diego courtroom into the hallway where jurors were standing around waiting. Suddenly he screamed and crashed to the floor. "He was out for about a minute," said the prosecutor. "It was very effective."

What the prosecutor was praising, the cause of Valdez's sudden collapse, was the accidental discharge of an electronic shock belt, popularly called a stun belt, which the defendant had chosen to wear under his clothing rather than appear in handcuffs and chains before the jury. Stun belts deliver 50,000-volt shocks to the left kidney, which fan out from there through blood channels and nerve pathways. Shocks can be administered by guards from a distance of 300 feet simply by the push of a button. This is one of the reasons why stun belts are so popular with police and correctional officials, especially those who oversee the increasing number of chain gangs and don't want to get near their prisoners to incapacitate them.

And incapacitate the belts surely do. An eight-second application of shock inevitably knocks a person to the ground and may induce urination, defecation, or unconsciousness. Manufacturers promote them as nonlethal alternatives to guns because they allegedly allow for effective control of prisoners without inflicting lasting damage. That is a major reason why the Federal Bureau of Prisons decided in 1994 to use stun belts in medium- and high-security lockups. Since then dozens of state and county officials have purchased them.

The stun belt is only one of the latest in a series of devices using electric shock that have been manufactured in the United States to provide law enforcement officials with what is advertised as a safe, convenient means of controlling and transporting prisoners. Stun guns, shock batons, electric shields, some of them using up to 250,000 volts on low amperage—these and many similar devices are becoming more and more commonplace in sheriffs' offices and prison guard stations across the country.

Unlike the traditional electric cattle prod, which causes intense localized pain, stun weapons are designed to temporarily incapacitate a person, inflicting agonizing pain throughout the body in a matter of seconds. One of the most popular, the Taser, which fires electrified darts connected to a wire, was first tested in 1969 by John H. Cover, Jr., and later became famous when it was used against Rodney King. Of those early tests, which he performed on himself, Cover says, "I . . . immediately knew that I had found what I was looking for—an electric shock that was harmless in terms of not killing or injuring—but made you 'TAKE NOTICE'—it was a MOOD Changer!!"[1] According to Cover, the National Rifle Association and "small arms gun lobby groups," apparently fearing Tasers would displace guns, tried to put the manufacturer out of business after it began marketing its product in 1975. But support from such satisfied customers as the Los Angeles Police Department (which had discovered that, among other things, shock batons took people on PCP "off their high" immediately) kept the company thriving.

As of 1995, though stun guns were reported to be illegal in Illinois, Hawaii, New Jersey, New York, Michigan, Massachusetts, and Rhode Island, and in some municipalities, they were used in many other states, including Oklahoma, Arizona, Florida, and Iowa, as well as by the federal government. At least forty US companies manufacture shock devices and not a few of them sell them overseas. While not alone in the market, the United States has a corner on the business.

Stun Tech, Inc.

One of the most prominent of those US companies is Stun Tech of Cleveland, Ohio, manufacturers of the popular electronic shock belt called R-E-A-C-T (for Remote Electronically Activated Control Technology). Stun Tech's basic information packet describes the name choice:

> For every action there is a R-E-A-C-Tion—basic physics. Therefore, activation of the belt would *only* be in response to a violent act, a choice made by the individual wearing the belt and acted upon by the attending control officer.[2]

The emphasis on the limited uses to which such a device should be put reflects Stun Tech's tacit recognition that it is peddling a product that could easily be used irresponsibly; it states, for example, that it will not sell belts without buyers participating in an indepth training program. "Note," the packet announces in bold print, "Any use of the R-E-A-C-T belt system for officer gratification, inmate punishment, torture or interrogation will result in criminal charges against that officer or agent." But how Stun Tech would ever know about such misapplication or find itself in a position to press charges against such "officers or agents" is hard to imagine. Dennis Kaufman, president of the company, recently said that he has sold some 1,100 stun belts to US law enforcement agencies, including 300 to the federal government;[3] he has acknowledged, however, that Stun Tech does no research on the prison systems to which it sells its products.[4]

If Stun Tech pays lip service to restraint, its other promotional statements make a point of its belt's crueler uses. One of the great advantages, the company says, is its capacity to humiliate its wearer. "After all, if you were wearing a contraption around your waist that by the mere push of a button in someone else's hand could make you defecate or urinate yourself," the brochure asks, "what would that do to you from the psychological standpoint?" And if the shock ever has to be administered? "One word—," brags the brochure, "DEVASTATION!"

The stun belt causes this result with only a one-second delay between the activation of the device by a guard and the onset of the eight-second shock. No doubt the brevity of the delay time helps to explain why the belt has been unintentionally activated by officials nine times. This was the result, Kaufman says, of operator errors, and after such errors were publicized, the company felt it had to install a switch guard on its belts so that the person controlling the belt could not casually flip on current. But no switch guard can offset the fact that the 50,000 volts can be administered in eight-second segments as frequently as the operator chooses; and no switch guard can mitigate the apparent propensity of human beings to inflict gratuitous pain upon their fellows—particularly if they can do so from a distance.

Cruelty made easy

Brutality is not difficult to document when it comes to guards' treatment of prisoners or police officers' behavior toward suspects, particularly racial minorities. Within the past ten months human rights groups have reported on apparent increases in the number of police shootings and the number of people who have died in custody in New York City, as well as the widespread occurrence of rape of women prisoners by male guards in eleven state prisons for women.[5]

Electronic shock weapons and particularly the stun belt differ from fists and clubs in that many of them require little physical contact between the operator and the recipient of the shock. Furthermore, most of them leave little, or no, evidence on the victims' bodies that any kind of coercive action has taken place. Unlike a gunshot wound, a bruise from a police club, or a rape, electronic shock usually provides investigators with little physical proof with which to corroborate charges of brutality. Since the shocks can be applied repeatedly, the only restraints on their sadistic repetition are the training, supervision, and ultimately the discretion of the officer involved. There is reason to suspect, however, that such discretion may decline in direct proportion to the increasing physical distance between operator and victim.

Among the most famous, if controversial, psychological tests ever performed in an American laboratory were those of a Yale psychologist, Stanley Milgram, who tried to measure the extent to which volunteer subjects would administer electric shocks to a victim if instructed to do so by an authority figure, in Milgram's case the experimenter.[6] Milgram found that a high percentage of people would continue to administer shocks even when they heard the recipient cry out in pain and beg them to stop. They were sometimes willing to continue even past the point when the victim (who was, unknown to the subjects, an actor) feigned unconsciousness. Milgram was criticized for being inconsiderate of his volunteer subjects, but his conclusions about their behavior were stark:

> With numbing regularity good people were seen to knuckle under the demands of authority and perform actions that were callous and severe. Men who are in everyday life responsible and decent were seduced by the trappings of authority . . . into performing harsh acts.

Police officers and prison guards work within a rigid structure of command. Milgram's experiments were widely criticized at the time, both on ethical and scientific grounds. But if he is even partially correct, the power of authority could either increase the abusive use of weapons if that were the order of superiors or, conversely, it could discourage such abuse if the commanding officers and officials took strong positions against it.

One little-remarked aspect of Milgram's study, however, suggests particularly alarming consequences when it comes to the use of stun belts. For Milgram also found that the more physically remote the victim from the subject, the greater the likelihood the subject would administer shock to a dangerous level. The farther away the shock victim, Milgram said, the "more difficult for the subject to gain a sense of *relatedness* between his own actions and the consequences of these actions for the victim."

The stun belt can be used from distances of up to 300 feet. It is designed exactly for circumstances in which guards want to control prisoners without getting near them. Indeed, one of the device's major selling points is that it provides guards with psychological dominance over prisoners because those prisoners can seldom be sure who is administering the shock or when or for what offense it might be delivered. In this sense, prisoners are unable to "read" the face or the body language of their potential shocker and, similarly, the officer need not look into the eyes of the victim. As Milgram put it, "It is easier to harm a person when he is unable to observe our actions than when he can see what we are doing." In courtroom use, two activating transmitters can be provided, one for the court officer and one for the judge, thus ensuring that a prisoner will be uncertain where his punishment is coming from. The stun belt appears to make it as easy as possible both emotionally and logistically to deliver a disabling jolt of pain.

Health risks of shock weapons

Is that jolt and those provided by other electronic shock weapons physically dangerous or can the manufacturers legitimately claim to have produced a safe, nonlethal control device? John Cover insists that "police use of Tasers has saved at least 20,000 lives, officers & criminals thus far. And all claims that it killed have been disproven. . . ."[7] One study, though, reported at least three deaths from cardiac arrest among some 218 patients brought to a Los Angeles emergency clinic between 1980 and 1985 after being shot by police with Taser guns. In these cases, the heart failure was caused by a sharp increase in the toxicity of the drug phencyclidine (PCP) which the patients had ingested. And in July 1996, a twenty-nine-year-old woman, Kimberly Lashon Watkins, died of cardiac arrest after being shot with a Taser by Pomona, California, police.[8]

One of the great advantages [of the stun belt] . . . is its capacity to humiliate its wearer.

Medical opinion on the effects of shock weapons is decidedly mixed. For one thing, as Tim McGreevy, an independent consulting engineer who has tested dozens of stun guns, points out, the effectiveness of such weapons depends upon many variables: not only the voltage but the kind of batteries used, the amount of energy delivered in each electrical pulse, the thickness of the clothing worn by the recipient, and the place on the body where the shock is applied. Manufacturers' claims about the effects of the peak voltage a device can deliver, McGreevy has concluded, are not a reliable indicator of a stun gun's performance, since testing a shock weapon's true effectiveness is difficult. "Most buyers do not wish to test the various models on themselves," McGreevy notes dryly, "and there is a dearth of volunteer subjects (particularly those who would volunteer to test 15 different models [of stun guns] and be shocked repeatedly with each one)."[9]

Stun Tech itself says that it has never conducted an independent study, with external referees, on its product.[10] In fact the only medical evidence of the belt's safety included in Stun Tech's information package is a letter from Dr. Robert A. Stratbucker of the University of Nebraska Medical Center reporting on the testing of the stun gun—not even the stun belt—on "anesthetized swine." He then concluded that the belt would be no worse, that is, "no more hazardous than properly *employed* older style stun devices, a hazard itself which has been previously proven to be trivial *under circumstances of proper usage.*"[11] [emphasis added]

Other physicians dispute the "trivial" impact of "older style stun devices." Dr. Armand Start, head of the National Center for Correctional Healthcare Studies and a former prison physician, challenges the claim that stun guns are harmless and cites studies that warn of possible respiratory arrest, ventricular fibrillation, heart pump failure, and cardiac arrhythmias, after only two to three seconds of shock, to say nothing of eight.[12] A 1990 study by the British Forensic Science Service reached similar conclusions,[13] and at least one death has been directly attributed to an electronic riot shield, ironically the death not of a prisoner but of a Texas corrections officer who had agreed to undergo two 45,000-volt shocks as part of a test and collapsed shortly afterward.[14]

What is clear is that electronic stun weapons, particularly the newer ones, have not been adequately tested to determine the long-term medical effects of such shocks, especially if they are applied repeatedly. And what virtually everyone, including most manufacturers, agrees on is that stun weapons should not be used on certain categories of prisoners. Peter M. Carlson, Assistant Director of the Federal Bureau of Prisons says that it is not the Bureau's policy to use stun belts on "1) pregnant female inmates, 2) inmates with heart disease, 3) inmates with multiple sclerosis, 4) inmates with muscular dystrophy, and 5) inmates who are epileptic."[15] But early pregnancy, heart disease, and cerebral or aortic aneurysms, among other diseases, are notoriously hard to spot on the basis of standard medical screening. And even the healthiest prisoners could sustain a life-threatening injury if they crashed to the ground unexpectedly.

Dangers of misuse abroad

Whatever the limitations of medical screening in American prisons, such screening cannot possibly take place before an arrest or during riot control—two situations in which shock batons and shields are frequently employed. Moreover, shock weapons have consistently been used by foreign regimes to inflict the most excruciating forms of torture upon their victims.

The use of electronic shock weapons for torture has been reported in at least eighteen countries, including Egypt, Mexico, Russia, Saudi Arabia, and perhaps most notoriously in China. In 1995, for example, Mexican security forces, particularly the state judicial police, were accused of torturing hundreds of prisoners of conscience and members of ethnic minorities through near-asphyxiation, forcing peppered water into the nose, and electric shocks.[16]

The stun belt appears to make it as easy as possible both emotionally and logistically to deliver a disabling jolt of pain.

In Saudi Arabia refugees from Iraq accused of spying for Saddam Hussein have been subjected to electronic torture. One of them described it this way:

> The secret police handcuffed me. . . . A bar was put between my legs. Then they started beating me up with the electronic sticks. For many hours they tortured me on the soles of my feet. Being hit with an electronic baton not only made me vomit but I lost control of everything. I lost control of my bowels, my water. . . . I was left in my own vomit and urine all night.

Torture with electronic equipment may be the most widespread in China where political prisoners report its repeated application to their ears, teeth, necks, armpits, inner thighs, and genitalia. Tibetan monks and nuns who are imprisoned for their peaceful advocacy of freedom for Tibet are some of those most consistently abused by electric torture. Palden Gyatso, a Tibetan monk who was imprisoned for thirty-three years, managed to smuggle Chinese torture instruments into India and, referring to an electronic baton, he said,

This is the worst thing. . . . If they press that button, your whole body will be in shock. If they do it for too long, you lose consciousness but you do not die. If they press this button, you can die. They used it all the time on my body.[17]

What is clear is that electronic stun weapons . . . have not been adequately tested to determine the long-term medical effects of such shocks.

Sale of electronic shock weapons is prohibited in Belgium, Luxembourg, the Scandinavian countries, Switzerland, and the United Kingdom. Are American companies supplying electronic weapons to countries that use them for torture? Remarkably enough, it is almost impossible to find out. The Commerce Department created in 1994 a separate export licensing category for "specially designed implements of torture," the apparent presumption being that any manufacturer honest enough to call a torture instrument a torture instrument would thereby be assured of being denied a license. But such instruments as stun guns, shock batons, and riot shields are categorized as "crime control" items and can be sold without restriction as "general merchandise."[18]

Between 1991 and 1993 the Department issued 2,083 licenses for the sale of "crime control equipment" valued at $117,300,000 to 106 countries; the Department refuses to say how much of this sum was paid for stun weapons. Reportedly, export of such equipment was approved last year to such countries as Mexico, Lithuania, Panama, and Tanzania, though the Commerce Department's confidentiality rules make it difficult to know for certain.[19]

If the Commerce Department's control of the export of thumbscrews is any measure, however, there is cause for concern. Thumbscrews are miniature handcuffs which are good for virtually nothing but inflicting pain. The Department has acknowledged approving an unspecified shipment of them to Russia last year. It will not say to whom in Russia it authorized the sale. The Department's own export license records for 1995 reveal, however, that it authorized the sale of "police helmets/handcuffs/shields used for torture" to Saudi Arabia, a country whose police are well known for their brutality.[20]

Just as worrisome, thumbscrews, blackjacks, and electronic weapons can be shipped legally under the category of general merchandise to NATO countries (including Turkey, where torture is a common practice), Australia, New Zealand, and Japan. Nor has the government required those who order and use such equipment to sign certificates that it would not be re-exported.[21] Amnesty International research shows that approximately forty US companies are manufacturing shock technology that could be exported and used for torture. Whether their equipment has fallen into the hands of torturers is at the moment impossible to know.

Protection from our worst selves

Article VIII of the US Bill of Rights prohibits "cruel and unusual punishment." The International Covenant on Civil and Political Rights to which the US is a party forbids torture and degrading treatment or punishment. Whether or not electronic shock falls into any of these categories depends at least in part upon ascertaining the full medical effects of its application, effects which are still under debate. Until a rigorous, independent medical review of electronic shock weapons is undertaken and it is shown that they do not contribute to deaths in custody or constitute ill-treatment according to both US and international standards, their use by government officials should be suspended.

In one respect the United States is already violating international guidelines. The United Nations Standard Minimum Rules for the Treatment of Prisoners expressly prohibit the use of restraints, such as the stun belt, on prisoners appearing before a judicial authority. This prohibition has been repeatedly violated, not just in the case of Edward Valdez but in others such as that of James Filiaggi. Filiaggi appeared before the Lorain County, Ohio, Common Pleas Court in 1995 wearing a stun belt. According to news reports, a deputy escorting Filiaggi into court accidentally set off the belt on the first day of the trial, causing Filiaggi to fall to the ground. After his conviction, his lawyer appealed, claiming that the shock incapacitated his client and rendered him incapable of helping with his defense. The appeal was denied.[22]

The use of stun belts on prisoners appearing in court should certainly be outlawed. And the United States should prohibit the sale of instruments which can potentially be used for torture or ill-treatment to any country with a clear record of such abuses. At the very least, all recipient countries should be monitored to ascertain the uses to which such exported equipment is put.

Until a rigorous, independent medical review of electronic shock weapons is undertaken . . . their use by government officials should be suspended.

It is hardly likely, however, that electronic weapons will ever be done away with altogether. In view of current national trends favoring more severe punishment of prisoners and the reintroduction of chain gangs, the odds seem strong that shock weapons will be used even more frequently in the years ahead. And there seems little prospect that their export will be effectively restricted. But it may not only be human rights groups and concerned medical doctors that are insisting that prisoners must not be subjected to devastating electric shocks, and that the restraint of prisoners should not lead to what may amount to an execution. The 20,000-member American Correctional Association has condemned the chaining of prisoners and similar practices as "harsh and mean-spirited," adjectives which might well apply to stun belts. The dangers of the misuse of stun weapons and of their accidental discharge against innocent citizens who are standing trial should be obvious. So should their potential for misuse by governments overseas.

Governments, moreover, are far from the only buyers of stun guns. As the market grows larger and competition among manufacturers increases, stun guns and electronic batons are being sold increasingly to private security companies and private citizens. It is even possible that they will be used by teachers to keep order in classrooms or by nurses to control the mentally ill in hospitals; and we may not be far from the day when carrying a stun gun in one's purse is as common as carrying a whistle or a can of mace is today.

If Stanley Milgram was right, large numbers of people cannot be trusted to use such instruments responsibly. That is all the more reason not only to prevent torture of potential victims but to protect the users of electronic instruments from their worst selves.

Notes

1. Letter from John H. Cover, Jr., to William F. Schulz, June 22, 1996.
2. Stun Tech, Inc., "A New Dimension in Suspect and Inmate Control: R-E-A-C-T Belt System Information Package," p. i.
3. See Peter Kilborn, "Revival of Chain Gangs Takes a Twist," *The New York Times*, March 11, 1997, p. A18.
4. Anne-Marie Cusac, "Stunning Technology," *The Progressive,* July 1996, p. 22.
5. Amnesty International, "Police Brutality and Excessive Force in the New York City Police Department," June 1996; and Human Rights Watch, "All Too Familiar: Sexual Abuse of Women in U.S. State Prisons," December 1996.
6. Stanley Milgram, *The Individual in a Social World: Essays and Experiments* (Addison-Wesley, 1977).
7. Letter from Cover to Schulz, June 22, 1996.
8. Amnesty International, "Arming the Torturers: Electric Shock Torture and the Spread of Stun Technology," March 1997, pp. 13 and 21.
9. Tim McGreevy, "Stun Guns: An Independent Report," 1994, T'Prina Technology, Aurora, Colorado, p. 1. See also Tim McGreevy, "Stun Guns: How Batteries Affect Power," *Law Enforcement Technology*, October 1995, pp. 110-111.
10. Cusac, "Stunning Technology," p. 21.
11. Stun Tech, Inc., "A New Dimension in Suspect and Inmate Control," Attachment.
12. Armand Start, M.D., "Amended Declaration," June 1996, pp. 121-127.
13. M.N. Robinson, C.G. Brooks, and G.D. Renshaw, "Electric Shock Devices and their Effects on the Human Body," *Medical Science and Law*, 1990, Vol. 30, No. 4.
14. Cusac, "Stunning Technology," p.18.
15. Letter from Peter M. Carlson to Wilder Tayler, Amnesty International, July 18, 1996.
16. Amnesty International, Annual Report, 1996, p. 224.
17. Amnesty International, "Arming the Torturers," pp. 8 and 11.
18. Michael S. Lelyveld, "Crime control or torture?," *The Journal of Commerce*, August 2, 1996, p. 1A.
19. Michael S. Lelyveld, "US sold torture tools to 6 nations," *The Journal of Commerce*, July 9, 1996, pp. 1A, 5A.
20. Amnesty International, "Arming the Torturers," p. 26.
21. Lelyveld, "Crime control or torture?," pp. 1A, 5A.
22. Stephen Hudak, "Shocking restraint," *Cleveland Plain Dealer*, Dec. 25, 1996, p. B7.

9

Prisoners Should Receive Humane End-of-Life Care

Nancy Neveloff Dubler

Nancy Neveloff Dubler writes for the Journal of Law, Medicine, and Ethics *and has been a board member and president of the American Society of Law, Medicine and Ethics, an organization dedicated to promoting high-quality scholarship, debate, and critical thought in law, health care, and ethics.*

With the public advocating longer prison sentences, the passage of "three strikes and you're out" laws, and the increasing numbers of prisoners infected with HIV, more inmates are dying in prison. Proper end-of-life care, including access to spiritual counseling, pain relief, and support from friends and family, collides with prison policies. These policies must be changed to provide end-of-life health care in prisons that is comparable to the care available in the surrounding community. Terminally ill prisoners whose infirmities render them no threat to society should be released so they can die peacefully in the community.

In 1997, the United States incarcerated over 1.7 million persons in local jails and in state and federal prisons.[1] These inmates are disproportionately poor and persons of color. Many lack adequate access to health care before incarceration and present to correctional services with major un-addressed medical problems.

Convictions for drug possession and use have increased the number of injection drug users with HIV and AIDS in prisons. Determinate sentencing and "three strikes and you're out" laws have increased the number of inmates who are aging and dying during their sentences. Their feelings reflect those of Larry Rideau, sentenced to life without parole and founder of *The Angolite*—an award-winning prison newspaper at Louisiana's Angola Prison—"The dream of getting out, you equate with heaven. Dying in prison you equate with hell."[2]

In the world outside the walls of correctional institutions, the last decade has seen substantial progress in accommodating the needs and wants of dying patients and their loved ones. Physicians, nurses, and social workers have enhanced their communication skills, facilitating open and honest discussion about diagnoses and prognoses even when the choices are difficult and the future dim. The use of advance directives permits decisionally capacitated patients to make present choices, including the appointment of health care agents to control their care in the future when they are no longer able to participate in decision making. The needs of dying patients for analgesia, physical comfort, and spiritual support are increasingly met by practices that reflect the evolution of hospice and palliative care. Protocols for addressing pain and relieving suffering are proliferating. Research on the dying process provides increasingly specific guidance on the least invasive and most supportive techniques that promote death with dignity.[3]

In spite of this progress, however, studies show that, even in the most advanced academic medical centers, many patients still die in pain.[4] Sobering data indicate that, despite concerted efforts to encourage the use of advance directives, it is rare to find any patient population where more than 25 percent actually sign a living will or a health care proxy appointment.[5] Many people who decline to execute advance directives see them not as a support for care, but as part of a systemic denial of care,[6] a finding with direct relevance to a discussion of health care delivery in prisons and jails. Patients who are old, of color, injection drug users, or infected with HIV are especially suspicious of the systems in which they receive care. Many of these patients are not interested in limiting care—they are interested in access to care.

Against this complex background are the more convoluted issues of care delivered in jails and prisons or in medical facilities related to these institutions. In contrast to nonincarcerated patients, inmates do not assume that the system is acting in their best interests. Dying prisoners may not be convinced that decisions to limit care and permit death have been preceded by the full range of efforts to extend and support life. Sadly, the problem lies not in their unfounded suspicions, but in the accuracy of their assessment.[7] In the nonincarcerated world, one important focus is on preventing overtreatment and inappropriately aggressive care at the end of life. In many correctional institutions, however, it is still necessary to ensure that inmate patients receive intensive care to extend life when that is medically appropriate.

Access to health services flows through the prison guards, which means it often may be impossible to distinguish between a refusal of care and a denial of care.

At a time when society is finally directing its attention to the importance of active palliation for terminally ill patients in hospitals and at home, it is still turning its face away from those it punishes. Moreover, this intolerable suffering will increase as the number of dying inmates grows unless intervention brings together in a mediative process all the stakeholders whose interests and responsibilities appear to conflict.

Decent end-of-life care in any setting requires a trusting alliance between care providers and patient, but forging an honest and supportive therapeutic relationship in prison is a formidable task. Despite the striving for independence of devoted medical care providers, a correctional institution's policies and procedures intrude on care plans. Access to health services flows through the prison guards, which means it often may be impossible to distinguish between a refusal of care and a denial of care.

This article argues that the obligations of care giving are not diminished when the setting is a correctional facility. After outlining the issues related to dying in prison, the discussion focuses on the end-of-life care that can and should be provided in the facility and supports the use of compassionate release programs. Finally, it suggests the need for a consensus process for determining the guidelines for and supporting the delivery of appropriate, effective, and principled care to those who, at the end of their lives, do not immediately evoke popular sympathy or concern.

Dying in prisons—increasing prevalence

Death is increasingly the final stage of a prison sentence for reasons having much to do with social and political priorities as with disease and illness. In addition to the myriad injuries and illnesses that afflict society, and the additional health problems that accompany high-risk lifestyles, prisons have become a repository for the AIDS epidemic. AIDS is intimately associated with injection drug behavior and American criminal policy has made determined efforts to incarcerate drug users. Non–drug users frequently contract HIV through unprotected sexual activity. Once in prison, the virus spreads. Not surprisingly, AIDS has become the leading cause of death in prisons and jails.[8] At the start of the AIDS epidemic, many prison officers and medical personnel were afraid to treat HIV-positive or AIDS-infected patients. Since then, absolute neglect of these patients has given way to decent treatment in some facilities and barely acceptable treatment in others.

The actual number of HIV-positive inmates and those with AIDS is difficult to identify. Most prison systems neither perform mandatory testing for HIV nor conduct anonymous serology surveys. A national survey conducted by the Bureau of Justice Statistics for the U.S. Department of Justice indicates 22,713 inmates infected with HIV in 1994, the most recent date for which the data have been compiled.[9] Consequently, the numbers reported—4,849 cases of AIDS for forty-seven state and federal prison systems in 1994—are clearly inaccurate, because they account mostly for those inmates who have already become symptomatic. Because the revised definition of the disease also encompasses a T-cell count below 200,[10] many more inmates now qualify as having AIDS, although they may not yet exhibit the opportunistic infections[11] that would bring them to the attention of the health services. Indeed, it is possible that the undercounting of HIV-positive inmates is a deliberate strategy of some systems to avoid the extraordinary cost of multiple drug therapy for asymptomatic individuals.

A more accurate picture of the frequency of AIDS in prison populations is provided by a blinded anonymous 1996 serology survey done in New York State. It shows that approximately 9,500 inmates were infected.[12] Because many inmates do not volunteer for confidential testing—

they fear the discrimination or segregation that may result if the disease were revealed—only anonymous surveys give a clear picture of the numbers of infected persons. Unfortunately, as treatment for AIDS becomes more sophisticated and preventive interventions more effective, the reluctance to submit to testing consigns many inmates to substandard care that may actually shorten their lives. This suspicion of the correctional health care system is precisely what works against the therapeutic alliance that is demanded for high quality end-of-life care.

Inmates . . . are rarely concerned about having their refusals of care honored; rather, they worry that they have been denied the care they want.

But inmates with AIDS do not represent the only segment of the prison population to die within correctional walls. In 1994, 2,888 males and 123 females died in federal and state correctional systems. Of those totals, 888 men and 35 women died of AIDS. The remainder died of other illnesses or natural causes, suicide, injury, execution, attack by another inmate, or unspecified cause. These numbers identify a most serious problem in the corrections system—close to 3,000 inmates died within a closed system under direct government supervision.[13]

The trend toward increased sentences and the proliferation of "three strikes and you're out" laws, determinate sentences, and mandatory minimums have combined with illness and injury to begin the "graying" of the prisons. Prisoners also tend to be physiologically older than their years would indicate. A prisoner aged fifty may be classified by society as middle aged; he may, in fact, already be an elderly person if many of his years have been spent in the prison system. Socioeconomic status and lack of access to preventive and acute medical and dental care may create as much as a ten-year aging differential.[14] Nationally, the number of inmates fifty-five and older more than doubled between 1981 and 1990.[15] Estimates are that the number of prisoners over age fifty will reach 125,000 by the year 2000, with 40,000 to 50,000 being over age sixty-five.[16] Given the hyper-aging phenomenon of the inmate population, many of these prisoners will be aged and infirm with multiple medical problems. These problems, if they mirror those in the general population, will include kidney failure, diabetes, cancer, heart disease, dementia, and the other degenerative diseases that fill geriatric practices and long-term care facilities.

Moreover, caring for an increasingly geriatric inmate population is likely to be extremely expensive. Estimates for the care of an elderly inmate range from $60,000 to $69,000 per year, in contrast to about $20,000 per year for a nonelderly, non-AIDS infected inmate.[17] The majority of these monies cover the cost of medical treatments and medications, special equipment for the handicapped, special education, recreation and work programs, prison hospital beds, and special facilities needed to protect the frail and elderly in the violent prison world.[18]

Medical care in prisons and jails

Absent effective and publicly accepted compassionate release programs, many prisoners will die in correctional hospitals and long-term care facilities. For these prisoners, one can argue that the judicial sentence they receive will be automatically converted to a sentence of life imprisonment without the possibility of parole. For inmates, as for many people, terminal illness is a time of great sorrow, loneliness, suspicion, pain, and suffering. The good death—an acceptance of the inevitable and a reconciliation with family and friends, supported by spiritual counselors in a comfortable surrounding—is rarely available inside prison walls. Plans for a good death often run afoul of prison rules and regulations, and are complicated by the structure of the medical care organization, the distance of families, and the barriers to communication and affection that exist in the punitive correctional environment.

In jails and prisons, death is always viewed as an event that will upset the inmate population or undermine security, concerns that are sometimes used to justify the suspension of rights protected for other members of society. The 1979 case of *Commissioner of Corrections v. Myers*[19] concerns an inmate's attempt to refuse dialysis, consistent with the well-settled right of capacitated adults to refuse unwanted treatment, even if that refusal hastens the patient's death.[20] In overruling the prisoner's refusal of treatment, the court noted that the interests of the state, as represented by the department of corrections, included "the preservation of internal order and discipline, the maintenance of institutional security, and the rehabilitation of prisoners."[21] These interests, the court held, permitted corrections officials to administer life-saving treatment without consent and over the specific objection of the inmate. This case and others have consistently placed the requirements of corrections administration over the rights of inmates to consent to or refuse treatment.

Care for a dying patient should not require a choice between care and comfort.

The *Myers* case, however startling, has little applicability to issues of terminal care in prison. Frail elderly inmates and those with cancer and AIDS are rarely concerned about having their *refusals* of care honored; rather, they worry that they have been denied the care they want and the support and comfort they need. Despite the ethical and legal imperative that decent prison and jail health care approximate the standard of care in the general community,[22] end-of-life care for the incarcerated almost always fails to reach that goal. Before proposing solutions, it is important to identify the issues.

What care should be provided?

Inmates, no less than other persons, should be provided with diagnostic and treatment interventions appropriate to their health needs. Yet, it is precisely at the end of life that the goals of medicine—to diagnose, comfort, and cure—and the mandate of corrections—to confine and punish[23]—clash most directly. The antagonism, suspicion, and fear that have governed the relationship between the inmate and authorities prior to the last stage of illness continue to define and constrain that relationship during the inmate's dying. For this reason, among others, compassionate release of dying inmates is such an important part of planning for terminal care.

Care for a dying patient should not require a choice between care and comfort. A mixed model should provide for all of the inmate's needs. Health care within the correctional institution must be guided by the same goals and standards that inform care in any other setting. When the illness or injury is responsive to therapy and the patient consents to treatment, a cure-oriented plan should be vigorously pursued. When the patient is clearly dying, however, and further treatment will only increase suffering without providing benefit or when the patient has refused further treatment, cure is no longer the goal. In these instances, the focus shifts and palliation becomes the priority of care, with the following considerations.

- Correctional and medical staff should be helped to regard and treat terminally ill inmates as patients approaching the end of life, not as individuals for whom suffering and dying are yet another appropriate phase of punishment.
- Palliative care protocols should be in place to ensure that the care team can accurately assess the level of physical discomfort and provide effective response. *An inmate's history of drug use should not be a disqualification from receiving adequate analgesia and even opioids when required for pain control.* (This provision challenges policies that exclude any narcotics from legal entry into a correctional facility.)
- The prison drug formulary should stock adequate pharmaceuticals, keeping them secure but available for the effective management of pain and other symptoms.
- Special foods and fluids should be made available on request, with assistance for those who cannot provide for themselves.
- Visiting rules should be relaxed to permit family members and other loved ones increased access to the patient.
- Chaplains and other spiritual advisors, including inmates, should also be permitted enhanced access to the inmate.
- Family members who have not been in contact with the dying inmate should be sought out for possible reconciliation or to make some provisions for the burial, avoiding the specter of a "potter's field" burial.
- Institutional rules should be relaxed to eliminate the requirement for dying patients to be shackled when moved outside the facility for consultation or treatment.
- Rituals to commemorate those who have died should be part of the prison culture of terminal care. Other inmates and even staff need to have some way of remembering those who have died. It can be especially numbing for staff to dispatch an ever-increasing number of inmates to the morgue.

Where should care be provided?

In an effort to streamline care, to gather trained staff, and to meet the needs of inmates, many correctional systems are developing special care units for dying patients. Many systems are experimenting with designated death units (DDUs) or hospice units to which terminally ill prisoners can be transferred at the end of life. Although a dedicated unit may seem reasonable, because staff can be trained in end-of-life care, and materials and equipment can be procured to meet individual needs, these units often turn out to be problematic rather than innovative.

Many prison physicians view DDUs or hospice as an alternative to aggressive treatment for possibly correctable medical problems. Patients with complex oncology problems or infectious disease syndromes, including AIDS, might be transferred to this unit rather than receiving specialty care from a fully trained expert. Good medical practice precludes assignment to a DDU until the patient has been examined and the case reviewed by a specialist in the field. This sort of review, *before* classifying the inmate as having a terminal and irreversible illness, should help to ensure that aggressive cure-oriented care is not discontinued prematurely.[24]

Not surprisingly, prisoners come to see transfer to the unit as a death sentence, which it very well may be. In a segregated facility, many dying inmates find themselves further away from their families and less accessible to the frequent visits a dying person craves. These terminal units are also likely to have special security classifications, making them less likely to offer educational and rehabilitation programs, to hold religious services, or to have access to the law library, all activities that enrich prison life at any stage.

Advance directives and other support for end-of-life care

Do-not-resuscitate orders (DNRs), living wills, and health care proxy agent appointments are increasingly part of advance planning to support decent end-of-life care. They can also be important in the correctional setting, with one major caveat: as noted above, it is very difficult, and in some settings nearly impossible, to distinguish between a refusal and a denial of care. If the inmate fails to arrive for a particular treatment, has he decided not to come or has the corrections officer at the gate denied him access to the medical unit? Has the inmate decided to see a visitor instead of the doctor, or has he/she been sent to an unexpected court appointment? The secluded nature of movement and the disparate power relationships within prisons can combine to permit the exclusion from care of inmates who have not chosen to reject care. This reality must inform the creation of instruments that are used prospectively to refuse care. These documents and the powers they represent are only legitimate if they truly reflect the values and preferences of the inmate and are in no way coerced or imposed by others.

With these caveats, advance directives can be invaluable to the dying inmate and his family. They can provide the basis for discussion of terminal care, including an outline of the issues that need to be addressed. They represent perhaps the final way for the inmate to exercise control in the present and for the future. They also provide important guidance for correctional authorities and should be used to permit the inmate to die in the facility rather than to be transferred at the end of life to a strange location without friends or familiar care providers. Continuity is one of the most crucial elements that decent terminal care can ensure. Remaining in the prison to die also avoids one of the greatest injustices—shackling the terminally ill inmate during transfer.

Living wills and health care agent appointments are legal instruments that allow a capable individual to articulate treatment wishes to be honored at a future time when the ability to make decisions might be lost. With some variation in policies and procedures, they are recognized in all fifty states and the District of Columbia.[25] Outside of prison, the appointment of an agent is generally preferable to a living will. It provides for a person who can discuss treatment options with the care team, weighing the benefits and risks in the light of the patient's current condition and prognosis. It assumes, however, that a person will be on the spot to discuss the issues and advocate for the dying inmate's wishes. As such, it is useful only if the correctional administration permits the agent to be at the site of care to participate in decision making and relaxes the visitation rules and administrative protocols that restrict the presence of noncorrectional personnel in the medical facility. Absent administrative flexibility, proxy agent appointments are not useful in the correctional setting. Without this cooperation and support, the decisions become nearly impossible, imposing a terrible burden on the agent. Under such circumstances, a living will may be a better choice for a patient concerned about controlling end-of-life care.

DNRs have also become part of the ethical armamentarium of providers of terminal care. They are appropriate for a terminally ill patient whose chances of surviving the resuscitation are slight and whose quality of life, if the resuscitation were successful, would be severely compromised. When an inmate authorizes a DNR, the danger is that some member of the care team or the administration has convinced him/her to refuse cardiopulmonary resuscitation when that would not have been the inmate's real choice. On the other hand, it should be of equal concern if inmates are not being offered the option to refuse resuscitation and are thus suffering the indignity and possible pain of an inappropriate aggressive intervention.

Compassionate care for the terminally ill is a difficult paradigm to create in a prison environment.

One way to address the concerns about freely chosen care plans for the terminally ill is to involve someone outside the prison structure in the process of discussion and decision. The most helpful person is likely to be the prison chaplain or a spiritual leader from the community. All these instruments and approaches, if used correctly to inform and empower the inmate-patient, can help structure end-of-life care in ways that the inmate finds most comfortable. If used oppressively only to streamline administration, they can further erode the dignity to which inmates and their families are entitled.

It is possible to find within the Americans with Disabilities Act (ADA)[26] some possible protection for the health care rights of dying prisoners.[27] Although it is clear that, outside of prisons, the elderly disabled and persons with AIDS are protected under the ADA, it is not so clear whether this legislation requires special accommodations for similar needs of these persons when they are incarcerated. Given the increasing judicial support for correctional administrative discretion, it would not be surprising if some or even most courts "elevate the penological interests of security and efficiency above the statutory rights [of inmates]."[28] This is especially important because it is far from clear that all prisoners would be considered qualified individuals under the terms of the Act.[29]

Compassionate release

On January 31, 1997, the Press Association reported that the Director General of the English Prison Service had "apologized publicly for the treatment of a terminally ill prisoner who was shackled to a bed until just three hours before he died."[30] The report could have come as easily from any correctional facility in the United States now housing the terminally ill. The inherent disjunction between the goals of medicine and the goals of corrections require a fundamental reworking of correctional policies and procedures to accommodate the needs of the dying. Compassionate care for the terminally ill is a difficult paradigm to create in a prison environment, and it requires constant tending to ensure that it does not revert to a more retributive and punitive model. Also, some persons may disagree that compassionate care is an appropriate goal. The increasing support for incarcerating greater numbers of persons for longer sentences, opposition to rehabilitation as a goal, and escalating numbers of persons sentenced to death may reflect a greater intolerance for criminal behavior and hence less tolerance for compassion.

One solution is compassionate release, an alternative that permits an inmate to die at home or in a noncorrectional facility. A compassionate release program identifies inmates who are dying and whose condition precludes their posing a threat to society. The physician works with the department of corrections, the district attorney, and a judge to document the medical case and to argue for release so the patient can die more peacefully in the community.

The compassionate release option may prove to be a key element in preparing for the onslaught of dying inmates that the next decade seems likely to produce. Making the most effective use of this method, however, will require thoughtful planning, careful structuring, and a change in thinking about dying prisoners. In many states, compassionate release programs are not truly designed to facilitate the timely release of inmates, and many programs have no identified advocate to guide the system toward that goal. As a result, the vast majority of inmates requesting release die before the process is completed. In addition, the current compassionate release programs are barely comprehensible and would be exceedingly difficult for the average inmate or family to negotiate.[31] One commentator concludes:

> The mechanisms for compassionate release of terminally ill prisoners now operating in the United States are many and varied. These mechanisms share some common features, and they certainly exist with a common purpose. It is unfortunate, therefore, that many of the compassionate release programs are inefficient in accomplishing these laudable humanitarian goals. It is of even greater concern that some jurisdictions and the federal system are essentially devoid of compassionate release mechanisms. The creation of systems

that operate expeditiously and fairly is essential for success in the endeavor to extend humanitarian assistance even to those we have imprisoned. Ultimately, society is served if our compassionate impulses can reach beyond the issues of crime and punishment to serve all people as human beings.[32]

An effective compassionate release process would be expensive, but it would cost many thousands of dollars less than providing adequate end-of-life care in the prison setting.[33] Such a program would also shift the costs from correctional health care budgets to Medicare and Medicaid, where they would be largely invisible. Although cost saving need not be the primary factor considered in evaluating any particular inmate for compassionate release, it should certainly be taken into account in creating and justifying the program itself. Compassionate release programs can provide better care in preferable settings.

Effective use of the compassionate release program would require:

- early identification of potential candidates;
- creation of a mechanism for family members to request consideration;
- appointment of an advocate for each applicant with powers to negotiate the process through the correctional, criminal, and judicial administrations; and
- an appeal procedure available to prisoners and their families if the application were denied at any point in the process.[34]

Proposed approach to creating change

In 1976, the U.S. Supreme Court declared that prison and jail inmates have a constitutionally protected right to health care while incarcerated. The decision in *Estelle v. Gamble*[35] reasoned that imprisoning an individual, preventing access to medical care, and then not providing that care resulted in precisely the cruel and unusual punishments the Eighth Amendment was designed to prohibit.[36] The Court held, therefore, that correctional institutions were constitutionally required to provide care that was not "deliberately indifferent to . . . the serious medical needs of inmates."[37] Since 1976, all federal circuits have struggled with the meaning of these terms in the face of the reality of correctional life. There are collected volumes of cases that challenge every aspect of health care in correctional institutions in every state and in the federal court system.[38]

In addition, litigation about end-of-life care has gained new momentum from two recent Supreme Court decisions. In *Washington v. Glucksberg*[39] and *Vacco v. Quill*,[40] the Court held that, although no constitutional right to physician assistance in committing suicide exists, there is a caregiver obligation to address pain and suffering at the end of life and, perhaps, even a constitutionally protected right to aggressive palliative care.[41] The Court made special reference to "vulnerable groups,"[42] especially those who are unable to ease their own suffering as they approach death. Nowhere are the meanings of compassion and vulnerability felt more acutely than in correctional institutions.

It would be counterproductive, however, to rely again on case-by-case advocacy in the federal courts for interpretation and enforcement of this new right to aggressive palliative care. Litigation is the least effective, albeit sometimes the only, means of establishing rights. Nonetheless, the therapeutic context and the dimension of end-of-life suffering demand a more direct and inclusive approach that will forge alliances of compassion across spaces of mutual distrust.

By definition, compassionate care requires deviation from the correctional norm whose goals are segregation, stigmatization, and punishment.

A strategy is called for that builds on the common interests, experience, and expertise of stakeholders who can be convened to identify the barriers to decent care and to fashion a set of pragmatic and humane policies and procedures that would receive community support. In a process to which all parties can subscribe, the focus must be on the development of practical and politically acceptable methods for health care providers, supported by correctional administrators, to identify and respond to the needs of dying inmates.

The goal is to create a therapeutic, administrative, and political framework that commands such broad-based lay and expert support that all institutional systems would be comfortable working within its parameters without concern about appearing soft on convicted criminals. The financing of end-of-life care in correctional settings is a function of state and federal budget allocations. During the past fifteen years, legislatures have been eager to fund capital costs without necessarily financing the operational costs that accompany the expanding prison population. Decent end-of-life care will only be created when a professional and moral consensus supports adequate public expenditures.

The goal of changing end-of-life care in correctional institutions will only be met by creating the moral and strategic space in which humane end-of-life care becomes feasible. At present, correctional administrators and medical providers have no standard that supports or facilitates compassionate care. By definition, compassionate care requires deviation from the correctional norm whose goals are segregation, stigmatization, and punishment. Dying inmates need increased medical attention, expanded visiting hours with family and clergy, access to special foods, and relaxation of routine restrictions. It would be difficult, if not impossible, for any one correctional facility, acting on its own initiative, to implement the number and quality of changes needed for humane care. If end-of-life care is offered in the facility, public perception and legislative oversight are likely to charge "coddling," and if prisoners are given compassionate release, these same critics are likely to decry a "danger to the public." The disregard for wellbeing that has led many systems to end education programs (the only intervention correlated with decreased recidivism rates) is unlikely to risk disapprobation of government and populace. Collaborative action across states with the support of nationally created and widely accepted standards will provide the principled framework within which any particular state or local system could improve care while defending its action against public and legislative challenges.

Notes

1. See F. Butterfield, "Prison Population Growing Although Crime Rate Drops: Sentencing Is One Factor, Justice Dept. Says," *New York Times*, Aug. 9, 1998, at 18 ("In a new report, the Justice Department said the number of Americans in local jails and in state and Federal prisons rose to 1,725,842 in 1997, up from 1.1 million in 1990.").

2. D.C. Anderson, "Aging Behind Bars," *New York Times*, July 13, 1997, at 28.

3. See, for example, American Board of Internal Medicine, *Caring for the Dying: Identification and Promotion of Physician Competency* (Philadelphia: American Board of Internal Medicine, 1996): at 11–18; V. Dubowitz, "Withdrawing Intensive Life-Sustaining Treatment—Recommendations for Compassionate Clinical Management," *N. Engl. J. Med.*, 336 (1997): 652–57; C.K. Cassel and B.C. Vladeck, "ICD-9 Code for Palliative or Terminal Care," *N. Engl. J. Med.*, 335 (1996): 1232–34; S. Wanzer et al., "The Physician's Responsibility Toward Hopelessly Ill Patients," *N. Engl. J. Med.*, 320 (1989): 844–49; J. Zerwekh, "Do Dying Patients Really Need IV Fluids?," *American Journal of Nursing*, 97 (1997): 26–30; and Council on Ethical and Judicial Affairs, American Medical Association, "Council Report: Decisions Near the End of Life,"*JAMA*, 267 (1992): 2229–33.

4. A two-year prospective observational study with 4,301 seriously ill patients hospitalized at five teaching hospitals in the United States indicated that "for 50% of conscious patients who died in the hospital, family members reported moderate to severe pain at least half the time." SUPPORT Principal Investigators, "A Controlled Trial to Improve Care for Seriously Ill Hospitalized Patients," *JAMA*, 274 (1995): at 1591.

5. See E.R. Gamble, P.J. McDonald, and P.R. Lichstein, "Knowledge, Attitudes, and Behavior of Elderly Persons Regarding Living Wills," *Archives of Internal Medicine*, 151 (1991): 277–80.

6. This notion about drug-using patients with HIV comes from Diane La Gamma. See Personal Communication with Diane La Gamma, J.D.A., Staff Attorney, Legal Aid Society, Volunteer Division, Montefiore Medical Center, Bronx, New York (Oct. 8, 1997).

7. See J.S. Ornduff, "Releasing the Elderly Inmate: A Solution to Prison Overcrowding," *Elder Law Journal*, 4 (1996): at 177. For a discussion of a series of cases upholding the minimum standard of care in prisons, see M.T. Russell, "Too Little, Too Late, Too Slow: Compassionate Release of Terminally Ill Prisoners—Is the Cure Worse Than the Disease?," *Widener Journal of Public Law*, 3 (1994): at 811 n. 43.

8. See L.A. Pagliaro and A.M. Pagliaro, "Sentenced to Death? HIV Infection and AIDS in Prisons—Current and Future Concerns," *Canadian Journal of Criminology*, 34 (1992): 201–14, cited in R.L. Braithwaite, T.M. Hammett, and R.M. Mayberry, *Prisons and AIDS: A Public Health Challenge* (San Francisco: Jossey-Bass, 1996): at 17. As one inmate stated, "Somehow they should not have to get the death sentence just because they have the habit." Braithwaite, Hammett, and Mayberry, *id.* at 116.

9. See P.M. Brien and A.J. Beck, *HIV in Prisons 1994* (Washington, D.C.: Bureau of Justice Statistics, NCJ 158020, 1996).

10. See "1993 Revised Clarification Systems for HIV Infection and Expanded Surveillance Case Definition for AIDS Among Adolescents and Adults," *Morbidity & Mortality Weekly Report,* Dec. 18, 1992.

11. "Opportunistic" refers to the nature of disease that is caused by an organism in a host with lowered resistance. See *Stedman's Medical Dictionary* (Baltimore: Williams & Wilkins, 26th ed., 1995): at 1255. Because of their compromised im-

mune systems, people with AIDS are particularly susceptible to infections caused by organisms that ordinarily would not jeopardize people without AIDS.

12. See M. Purdy, "As AIDS Increases Behind Bars, Costs Dim Promise of New Drugs," *New York Times*, May 26, 1997, at Al.

13. See J.M. Brown et al., *Correctional Populations in the United States, 1994* (Washington, D.C.: U.S. Department of Justice, July 1996): at 85.

14. See J.B. Morton, *An Administrative Overview of the Older Inmate* (Washington, D.C.: U.S. Department of Justice, 1992): at 4.

15. See Youth and Special Needs Program Office, Florida Department of Corrections, *Status Report on Elderly Inmates, 1993* (Tallahassee: Florida Department of Corrections, 1993): at 5, cited in W.E. Adams Jr., "The Incarceration of Older Criminals: Balancing Safety, Cost, and Humanitarian Concerns," *Nova Law Review*, 19 (1995): at 469 n.22.

16. See S. Chaneles, "Growing Old Behind Bars," *Psychology Today*, 21, no. 10 (1987): at 47, 49, cited in Adams, *id.* at 470.

17. See Ornduff, *supra* note 7, at 174–75, esp. n.16.

18. See J.H. Wright Jr., "Life Without Parole: An Alternative to Death or Not Much of a Life at All?," *Vanderbilt Law Review*, 43 (1990): at 563, cited in Ornduff, *supra* note 7, at 174 n.12.

19. *Commissioner of Corrections v. Myers*, 379 Mass. 255, 399 N.W.2d 452 (1979).

20. See *id.*

21. *Id.* at 457.

22. See N.N. Dubler, ed., *Standards for Health Services in Correctional Institutions* (Washington, D.C.: American Public Health Association, 2nd ed., 1986).

23. See N. Dubler and B.J. Anno, *Ethical Considerations and the Interface with Custody. Prison Health Care: Guidelines for the Management of an Adequate Delivery System* (Washington, D.C.: U.S. Department of Justice, National Institute of Corrections, Grant No. 88P02GHB0, 1991): at 53.

24. Many of the ideas expressed in this section are derived from discussions. See Personal Communication with Robert L. Cohen, M.D., Assistant Professor of Social Medicine and Clinical Epidemiology, Albert Einstein College of Medicine, Bronx, New York (Apr. 1997); and Personal Communication with Staff Members, Prisoners' Rights Project, New York Legal Aid Society, New York, New York (Apr. 1997).

25. See C.P. Sabatino, *Health Care Surrogate Decision-Making Legislation* (Washington, D.C.: American Bar Association, Commission on Legal Problems of the Elderly, Jan. 1998): at 1–5 (unpublished); and H.S. Margolis, M.G. Gilfix, and C.P. Sabatino, "Health Care Decision Making in an Elder Law Practice," in H. Margolis, ed., *The Elder Law Portfolio Series* (New York: Aspen Law & Business, Portfolio 16, Release 8, June 1997): at App. 16-95 to -108.

26. See Americans with Disabilities Act, 42 U.S.C. S 12117 (Supp. II 1990).

27. A U.S. Supreme Court case, *Pennsylvania Department of Corrections v. Yeskey*, 118 S. Ct. 1952, 66 U.S.L.W. 4481 (1998), decided in June 1998, held that the Americans with Disabilities Act's "language unmistakably includes state prisons and prisoners within its coverage."

28. I.P. Robbins, "George Bush's America Meets Dante's Inferno: The Americans with Disabilities Act in Prison," *Yale Law and Policy Review*, 15 (1996): at 62.

29. See *id.* at 54.

30. Press Association Newsfile, Jan. 31, 1997, at 412–14.

31. See 18 U.S.C. SS 3582(C)(1)(A), 4205(G) (1994).

32. Russell, *supra* note 7, at 836.

33. See *id.* at 804.

34. See N.N. Dubler and B. Heyman , "End-of-Life Care in Prisons and Jails,"

in M. Puisis, ed., *Clinical Practice in Correctional Medicine* (St. Louis: Mosby, 1998): at 359–64.

35. *Estelle v. Gamble*, 429 U.S. 97 (1976).

36. See *id.*

37. *Id.*

38. See Ornduff, *supra* note 7, at 177; and Russell, *supra* note 7, at 811 n.43.

39. *Washington v. Glucksberg*, 117 S. Ct. 2258 (1996) (State of Washington's prohibition against "causing" or "aiding" a suicide does not violate the Due Process Clause of the Fourteenth Amendment of the U.S. Constitution).

40. *Vacco v. Quill*, 117 S. Ct. 2293 (1996) (State of New York's prohibition on "assisting" suicide does not violate the Due Process Clause of the Fourteenth Amendment of the U.S. Constitution).

41. See R.A. Burt, Sounding Board, "The Supreme Court Speaks: Not Assisted Suicide but a Constitutional Right to Palliative Care," *N. Engl. J. Med.*, 337 (1997): 1234–36.

42. 117 S. Ct. at 2273.

10

Chain Gangs Should Be Abolished

Tracy L. Meares

Tracy L. Meares is an assistant professor at the University of Chicago Law School and contributes columns regularly to U.S. Catholic.

Chain gangs originated in the late nineteenth century as a mechanism to keep African Americans in servitude after emancipation. Today, the use of chain gangs by prisons bears a disturbing similarity to slavery, especially since African Americans comprise a large percentage of the prison population. Chain gangs are inhumane, and have little effect reducing crime, the costs of imprisonment, and recidivism rates.

Imagine the following scene: it's a hot summer day. The sun is beating down on African-American men. They are shackled to each other as they chop weeds for 12 hours. Armed guards and panting dogs watch intently over the chained men.

One may think that this imaginary scene is rendered in the sepia tones of history. It is not. Chain gangs, unfortunately, have become an increasingly common part of the American landscape. Chain gangs are a reality in at least seven states, and they are imminent in several more. Moreover, chain gangs are not confined to Alabama, the self-proclaimed heart of Dixie, and other former states of the Confederacy. Wisconsin, Michigan, Iowa, and Maryland—Union states all—have decided to welcome displays of shackled prisoners along state highways.

Let there be no mistake about it, there is an unambiguous historical connection between chain gangs and slavery. Advocates of the modern chain gang in Southern states trade on this historical connection. Anyone who disagrees need only consider the comment of one Alabama roadside chain gang spectator: "I love seeing 'em in chains. They ought to make them pick cotton."

Reprinted from "Let's Cut Chain Gangs Loose," by Tracy L. Meares, *U.S. Catholic*, July 1997, with permission from *U.S. Catholic*, Claretian Publications, www.uscatholic.org, 800-328-6515.

History of chain gangs

At the beginning of this century chain gangs were used as a mechanism to keep African Americans in voluntary servitude even after Emancipation. Southern judges commonly sentenced African Americans convicted of vagrancy (also known as unemployment) or loitering to time on the chain gang, where iron shackles were welded to an offender's ankles, and dogs, whips, and starvation were used liberally. Nor was a chain gang sentence limited to those convicted of petty crimes. In many cases mere breach of a contractual obligation was enough for a chain gang sentence. Contract-enforcement laws directed primarily at African American farm laborers transformed labor contracts into slavery. These laws made it a criminal offense for a farm laborer to quit a yearlong job for a better job at a higher wage. African American laborers were forced to choose between working out the original low-wage contract or spending several months of forced, brutal labor on a chain gang where fatality was not uncommon.

Little has changed

Though contract-enforcement laws are now unconstitutional relics of the past, the racial disparities in state prison populations have not changed. African Americans comprise about half—in Alabama, Georgia, and Maryland well over half—of the incarcerated prisoners in almost every state that has sanctioned the modern chain gang. (Iowa, with an African American prison population of 25 percent, is a notable exception.) These numbers mean that slavery's image is an inescapable aspect of the return of chain gangs.

The obvious costs of resurrecting a punishment so intimately connected with American slavery clearly outweigh any benefit American citizens can expect to gain. Aside from the very clear problems associated with the historical symbolism of the chain gang, there is a more basic problem. No one can convincingly argue that chain gangs will effectively reduce crime.

Chain gang proponents often express a desire to make prison so awful that a prisoner would not ever consider coming back. One must wonder how many legislators have been inside a state correctional facility. Prison already is not a pleasant place, as anyone who actually has been inside one can attest. Chain gang proponents also argue that the public humiliation of service on a chain gang will lower recidivism and may even deter law-abiding folks from considering a life of crime. This argument assumes that little-to-no humiliation is associated with going to prison—clearly a ridiculous idea. It is extremely unlikely that humiliating service on a chain gang will advance the deterrent value that we already obtain through imprisonment.

Adding chain gangs to imprisonment is not a cheap way to purchase an additional measure of deterrence. Obviously chain gang service does not make imprisonment any less expensive. Legislators who advocate chain gangs as a shaming penalty need to think again. If shaming penalties are useful at all, they are useful for their potential to serve as alternatives to incarceration. But chain gang advocates usually propose to apply chain gang service to those already incarcerated. No one discusses using chain gangs to make probation or community service more harsh. The legislators who propose chain gangs as shaming penalties are simply throwing more money at an already expensive program.

Chain gang service makes imprisonment more expensive while reducing the public's safety. We do not send offenders to prison simply to deter them from committing offenses when they are released. We send offenders to prison to incapacitate them and protect the public. Removing prisoners from the confines of prison walls and requiring them to work along roadsides increases the chances of escape, as Alabama learned in January 1996 when two prisoners escaped from a chain gang. The risk to the public from chain gangs could be reduced by making sure that only very "safe" prisoners (embezzlers?) are allowed to work outside the prison; however, most chain gang proponents would resist this approach.

The obvious costs of resurrecting a punishment so intimately connected with American slavery clearly outweigh any benefit American citizens can expect to gain.

Proponents call for more harsh treatment of violent and repeat offenders as a measure to reduce crime and protect the public, but they simply cannot have it both ways. They can either decide to keep so-called "incorrigible prisoners" behind prison walls, or proponents can attempt to make punishment more harsh for these offenders by requiring them to work outside in chain gangs. The most sensible option is obvious.

Education and training are better options

Why is there such a rush by lawmakers to drag these anachronistic punishments to the 21st century when numerous studies indicate that high school education and vocational training of prisoners is directly correlated with lower recidivism rates? It makes little sense to invest in an untested, morally ambiguous plan when that money would be much better spent on programs that can prepare a prisoner for the life he or she will lead outside. A life that will require a released offender to have basic reading and writing and maybe even computer skills. A life that is extremely unlikely to require an offender to know how to break rocks or chop weeds by the side of the road.

Perhaps lawmakers might support a policy that combines sound research and political appeal. How about this idea: Let's chain all inmates to desks and force them to learn to read and write. How about a bill to require that all inmates receive a General Equivalency Diploma? Granted we wouldn't be able to gawk at inmates learning in a classroom—like we can when driving by prisoners shackled together on the highway. True, we wouldn't be able to laugh at prisoners flexing their minds at their desks as we do now when humiliated criminals build up their muscles swinging picks at the taxpayers' expense. ("See, son, that illiterate prisoner sure is gettin' what he deserves, havin' to learn to read and all" probably isn't what chain gang proponents have in mind.) Of course, we wouldn't be able to have second and third chances at humiliating these recidivists because educated prisoners might actually become contributing citizens rather than repeat performers.

How about this idea: Let's chain all inmates to desks and force them to learn to read and write.

But such an approach might actually reduce crime, which is what the push for chain gangs is supposed to be about. Lowering recidivism rates, deterring crime, and allowing human beings to retain some semblance of dignity are the true goals of imprisonment. Humiliation of prisoners that depends on our country's sad history of enslavement of human beings is not. The argument against chain gangs is about more than preserving the humanity of prisoners. It's about preserving the humanity of the citizens of the United States. Every single one of us is degraded by the trend to bring back this ignominious punishment.

As Christians, we have an obligation to take a stand against morally outrageous punishments such as the chain gang. The gospels teach us to lead others by example, not to follow them blindly. It is time for us to move forward into the 21st century. It is time to repudiate chain gangs once and for all.

11

Sexual Abuse of Women Inmates Is Widespread

Nina Siegal

Nina Siegal is a freelance journalist who lives in New York. She writes for a variety of publications, including Ms., San Francisco Magazine, New York Times, *and* Progressive.

The vast majority of incarcerated women are subjected to sexual abuse on a regular basis. Some guards and administrators assume that when women are imprisoned they also give up the freedom to say no to sexual advances. Female inmates should be provided with a confidential forum where they can report abuse without fear of reprisal. The perpetrators must be prosecuted and the victims must be compensated for the pain and suffering they experienced as a result of the abuse.

Robin Lucas was asleep on a rickety bunk on Sept. 22, 1995, when she heard the steel door click and saw the silhouettes of three large men entering her cell. Before she could make out their faces, they had forced her arms back and handcuffed her from behind. Then they were upon her. They beat, savagely raped and then sodomized her for hours. When they got up to leave, one of the men stopped, retraced his steps and urinated on Lucas' brutalized body.

Lucas had self-surrendered at the Federal Correctional Institution for women at Dublin, Calif., on Feb. 24, 1994, prepared to serve a 30-month sentence for conspiracy to commit bank fraud. That morning, she had gotten up, taken her last bath, put on blue jeans and desert boots—a friend advised her to wear sturdy shoes—and entered her kitchen, where family members were arguing about what to make for her last breakfast. She felt a pang of joy as her relatives assembled around her, and she told them not to worry, everything was going to be OK.

"My whole attitude was positive," says Lucas. "I looked at this as a time for me to grow, to better myself, to learn all I could learn while I was there, to get physically fit and to come home and put that behind me and move on. That's how I looked at it—an extended version of summer camp."

Reprinted, with permission, from "Locked Up in America: Slaves to the System," by Nina Siegal. This article first appeared in *Salon.com*, at www.Salon.com. An online version remains in the *Salon* archives.

In many ways, it was like summer camp. Lucas spent the first 17 months in lightweight federal lockups, first at FCI Dublin, then at Geiger in Spokane, Wash., and then back to Dublin to the minimum-security facility next to the FCI, known as Camp Parks. She worked as a landscaper, electrician and clerk in the prison commissary, drove trucks and forklifts and cut hair in the prison salon. Although she was earning 12 cents to 29 cents an hour, substantially less than the $40 hourly wage she'd been making at the hair salon she owned before her conviction, it was OK with Lucas. "I was just doing my time," she says. Prison officials treated her like a model inmate, allowing her to work unsupervised outside the prison during the day.

The vast majority of . . . women in U.S. prisons and jails today have been exposed to some form of sexually related intimidation or assault by correctional officers.

But in August 1995, at Camp Parks, Lucas got into a fight with another inmate, and because the camp didn't have its own lock-down, she was sent across the street to the men's Federal Detention Center and placed in a special housing unit, familiar to all inmates as "the hole." She was locked in her cell 23 hours a day; her neighbors on either side were male inmates awaiting trial or sentencing for violent crimes, such as domestic violence, sexual assault and murder. It was there, in the 18th month of her sentence, that Lucas' nightmare began.

The atmosphere in the men's detention center was vastly different from that in the women's camps. Few, if any, female officers were assigned to the unit, and all aspects of Lucas' private life, including showering, using the toilet and changing her clothes, were exposed to the male guards and other prisoners. Male inmates were allowed to roam the corridors and harass Lucas and the few other women detained at the center, propositioning her with offers of contraband such as alcohol and drugs in exchange for sex. Lucas refused, and tried to pass the hours reading books and planning her life after prison.

On her third night in the hole a guard opened her cell door and let a man inside. The setup was immediately clear, and as the man moved toward her, Lucas put up a fight. He smashed her head against a wall, cutting open her forehead, and, afraid of the blood, he fled. There was no way of telling time in the hole, and Lucas didn't know how many days or weeks passed before the second attack. This time, a man climbed into her bed. Luckily, she was able to fend him off too.

She made a complaint to the facility's captain, who asked her to write an affidavit fingering the men involved. She requested an immediate transfer, but nothing happened. No one moved her out of the hole, no one took the key from the guard, no one protected her. Instead, someone leaked her statement to her assailants. Then came the Sept. 22 attack. Throughout it the three men threatened her life, called her a "snitch" and told her to "keep her mouth shut."

Lucas and I are sitting on the cold concrete basement floor of a board and care facility for the developmentally disabled she now manages in

Tiburon, Calif., as she assembles a gleaming new lawn mower she bought to tame the property's few patches of green. It is in this concrete room with a low stucco ceiling, and two file boxes filled with letters from friends in prison, that Lucas feels most at home. An African-American woman with eyes set wide apart, kinky hair cropped short, broad shoulders and an expression that is by turns stern and personable, Lucas speaks with a deep, steady voice.

"I'm still institutionalized in some ways," she says, standing and crossing to a desk placed diagonally between two concrete walls. "Four o'clock was count at the prison, and I still sometimes stand up then." There are many habits of prison life as well as memories that will fade over time, but others, like the assaults, will be impossible to forget. "I made a mistake that cost me 30 months of my life," she says, "but I'll be doing that time for the rest of my life."

A system saturated with abuse

There are some 78,000 women in more than 170 state and 10 federal prisons for women nationwide, plus another 60,000 who are doing time in thousands of county jails across America. Perhaps Lucas' story seems like an extreme example of custodial misconduct, but attorneys who work with incarcerated females say that the vast majority of the more than 138,000 women in U.S. prisons and jails today have been exposed to some form of sexually related intimidation or assault by correctional officers while serving their time. This means rape; it means coerced sex in exchange for cigarettes, tampons or phone calls to their kids; it means guards who stand outside showers, cells and bathrooms leering and making lewd remarks about the women's bodies; it means guards who stop women in the halls, in the cafeteria, on the yard to perform pat-searches that include groping of breasts and groins; and it means guards who corner women to conduct strip-searches 30 times a day.

> *The sheer magnitude of the problem [of sexual abuse in prisons] is hard to fathom.*

The horrors of life in men's prisons are already part of our common currency—prison fights, riots, prison gangs, inmate-on-inmate rape, the threat of contracting HIV. Our lens on women's prison has a softer focus, largely contrived by B movies in which tough, curvy broads with sharp tongues and snake tattoos start cat fights in the cafeteria. A few trays are thrown and peas tossed, but in the end, the matronly guards restore the order. It's titillating, lurid, harmless. The truth, of course, is much more alarming.

When women enter prisons and jails they essentially become invisible. Statistically, women inmates are much less likely to be visited by their friends and family, in part because their facilities are in remote locations. Women have less money at their disposal than most men when they enter prison, since the crimes that land them in prison in the first place—drug offenses, theft and welfare fraud—are crimes of poverty. Slave wages for their labors behind bars don't help them achieve any level of self-sufficiency, even to buy basic goods like aspirin or toothpaste. Stripped of their rights, money and contact with the outside world, they are powerless, helpless and easy to manipulate. Add male guards, with little training and absolute power, to that equation, and you've got a potentially lethal combination. Unless the prison administration takes an organized, active role in discouraging sexual misconduct, it is known to run rampant. And why not? No one is watching. The inmates have no reliable means of voicing complaints. And even if they did, who is going to believe the word of a convicted felon over a correctional officer anyway?

As a result, women behind bars are saddled with an added level of punishment, which is, of course, not sanctioned by any prison system, but is so overlooked and so common as to be essentially institutionalized.

The sheer magnitude of the problem is hard to fathom. "I have never worked with a single woman in prison or jail who has not reported some form of sexual harassment or abuse," said Ellen Barry, who has spent 20 years working as an attorney and advocate for inmates and is now co-chair of the National Network for Women in Prison and director of Legal Services for Prisoners with Children in San Francisco. "Sexual abuse and a climate of sexual terror—the fear of being daily harassed and assaulted by male guards—is pervasive throughout the entire prison system."

Fighting back

Lucas and two other Dublin inmates, Valerie Mercadel and Raquel Douthit, filed a class-action suit in U.S. District Court in August 1996, alleging that they were "sexually assaulted, physically and verbally sexually abused and harassed, subjected to repeated invasions of privacy and subjected to threats, retaliation and harassment when they complained about this wrongful treatment." They sought unspecified damages and changes to correctional procedures and staff training to protect other inmates. Lucas was released from prison in July 1996 and returned to her home in Tiburon. The other two women were transferred to different facilities. These three women's highly publicized, successful suit has helped bring some of the most lurid forms of abuse to light, but there are many women who've been subjected to similarly horrendous acts, whose voices we've never heard.

I just felt so sick because the truth was that he could do anything he wanted, and nobody was going to believe me.

Hundreds, perhaps thousands, of other women represented in class-action suits across the nation have similarly horrific stories. Right now, the U.S. Department of Justice has two federal suits pending against the departments of corrections in Michigan and Arizona, alleging sexual misconduct on a broad scale in their facilities. In recent years, similar legal actions have been brought on the state and county level against the District of Columbia, Colorado, Louisiana, Georgia, Washington state, California and the jail system in Santa Clara County, Calif.

In December 1996, Human Rights Watch, the international human rights watchdog agency, published a report called "All Too Familiar: Sexual Abuse of Women in U.S. State Prisons." It painted a grim picture of life in 11 state women's prisons in the District of Columbia, California, Georgia, Illinois, Michigan and New York. "We found that male correctional employees have vaginally, anally and orally raped female prisoners and sexually assaulted and abused them," states the report. "We found that in the course of committing such gross misconduct, male officers have not only used actual or threatened physical force, but have also used their near total authority to provide or deny goods and privileges to female prisoners to compel them to have sex or, in other cases, to reward them for having done so."

The findings and recommendations of the Human Rights Watch report were so scathing, in fact, that they prompted a rare visit by the United Nations rapporteur on Human Rights, who began a tour of America's women's prisons on May 20, 1998, to look into sexual abuse of women behind bars.

Brenda V. Smith, senior counsel and director of the Women in Prison Project of the National Women's Law Center in Washington, D.C., said the U.N. investigator will find substantial evidence of violations of inmates' civil and human rights. [The UN completed its investigation in December, 1998, and found much evidence of rights violations. They then published a report calling for widespread prison reform.] "I would say that every jurisdiction has a problem with it," she says, "and to the extent that they say they don't have a problem it is a problem." Again and again, those who have investigated conditions in women's prisons walk away with the same conclusion: In women's state and federal prisons, and in women's jails nationwide, sexual misconduct, assault and harassment are ubiquitous and persistent facts of life.

Legal problems

One might ask why men are hired as correctional officers in female facilities at all. Ironically, one of the reasons cited most often is equal opportunity employment. If men were forbidden from working in female institutions, would that limit women's employment in the men's prisons, which make up 94 percent of all prisons nationwide? In the 1970s, female prisoners in New York state filed suit against the department of corrections, arguing that male guards should not be stationed in women's units at night, or be allowed into certain other private areas of the prison. Attorneys for the case, however, stopped short of arguing that men should be barred from working in women's prisons altogether.

"We felt it was a balancing act between the 14th Amendment right to be free from employment discrimination vs. the First Amendment right and Eighth Amendment right to be free from cruel and unusual punishment," said Barry.

Another part of the answer arises from the weird logic of sexual politics behind bars: Some advocates for women in prison argue that some interaction with men, as long as it is tightly regulated, is better for female inmates' long-term well-being than no contact at all with the opposite sex. Other advocates say they are increasingly frustrated by those arguments.

Debra LaBelle, the lead attorney on a Michigan suit against the department of corrections, said she has now decided that men should be prohibited from working in female facilities, because no matter how much training and investigation is done to cut down on misconduct, the cases of harassment and abuse continue to pile up. "I resisted going there for a long time, but now I don't know another solution," she says.

Attorneys such as LaBelle chafe at the fact that in some states—14 to be exact—it is still not even illegal for guards to engage in sexual activity with inmates. Twenty-seven states and the District of Columbia expressly criminalize sex or "sexual touching" between prison staff and inmates, according to Widney Brown, a researcher with the Women's Rights Division of Human Rights Watch, while many of the remaining states dictate only that guards not be "over-familiar" with prisoners, a law that is extremely vague and difficult to enforce.

California, which boasts the largest number of incarcerated women in the nation, and the world's two largest women's prisons, criminalized sexual contact by guards with prisoners in 1994. But female inmates will tell you that hasn't done much to change the way guards in the state—more than half of whom are men—treat women in their custody.

Humiliation and degradation

Elly Cruz wears her dark brown hair in layers shrouding her large brown eyes, button nose and mouth neatly lined with maroon lipstick pencil. She sits uncomfortably, hands tucked between her crossed knees, in the downtown San Jose, Calif., office of Amanda Wilson, a civil rights attorney who helped her file suit against the Santa Clara County Department of Corrections in August 1996.

If anything, the problem is only becoming worse as the ranks of incarcerated women swell at an alarming rate.

Soon after she arrived at the jail, in January 1995, one of the correctional officers told Cruz that he "liked" her. This was not news. The guard often followed her on the yard. He had obtained her home phone number from her custody file and memorized it. He watched her shower at least 14 times and hovered over her while she slept at night. Cruz informed the captain and several officers, and asked to be transferred. She was moved to another part of the jail—but then he was too. He continued to pursue and harass her, physically restraining her several times to share his sexual fantasies, forcing her to play weird little word games that demanded that she answer with sexually explicit terms. Although Cruz didn't rebuff him outright, since he wielded a gun and a baton, she kept her distance. But that didn't work.

"He started getting angry, and I started getting scared," says Cruz, her bottom lip beginning to quiver. She canvassed prison staff for support, asked repeatedly to be moved again and told her friends to make sure that she was never alone. But one day, he cornered her, grabbed her by the arm, handcuffed her to a door and pushed her to the ground. Then he stood over her and, with a steely voice, said, "I can do anything I want to you, don't you know that?"

Then he let his hands roam free. "I just sat there with my hands behind me, I just went blank, I didn't even feel him touching me," she says, beginning to cry. "I felt so sick, I just felt so sick because the truth was that he could do anything he wanted, and nobody was going to believe me."

Cruz was finally moved—to the adjacent men's jail. There, she was in lock-down while male inmates passed her cell and watched her whenever they wanted. She later became the lead named plaintiff in *Cruz vs. Vasquez*, a class-action suit against the Santa Clara County Department of Corrections, alleging "a pattern and practice of sexual assaults, intimidation, abuse, threats of violence, sexual harassment and other violations of law." The case was settled in 1996, and the court ordered several changes in jail policy and facility design. But little has changed, says Wilson, whose law firm, the Public Interest Law Firm, recently filed a request to add another 50 plaintiffs to the suit.

Although many women, like Lucas and Cruz, suffered violence in isolation, their experience is one that's shared by many female inmates, both individually and in groups. At the Santa Clara County Jail, for example, scores of women have been repeatedly humiliated in mass strip-searches set up by male guards or with male guards looking on. Donna, a former inmate who did not want her last name used, describes such a search: "You're brought into a room, and there's a big window so the guards can see you," she says. "There are four or five women and you're all lined up and made to disrobe. If you happen to be menstruating, that's too bad. You'll just have to bleed on yourself until this is over. Then they say, open your mouth, lift up your tongue, pull your hair back, pull your ears forward. Put your hands forward, expose your underarms, expose the palms of your feet, squat, cough three times, stand up and bend over at the waist, expose your buttocks and vaginal area and then stand there until they tell you to get dressed."

At the Santa Clara jail, women were also pulled out of lineup and strip-searched in this way in full view of kitchen workers, grounds crews and even visiting attorneys and relatives. Prison officials say these searches are necessary to rout out contraband, but civil rights attorneys say their primary purpose is intimidation. "It's about power," says Wilson. "And because of the lack of response [from higher-ups], guards seem to have the attitude that they can do anything."

Walls of silence

Rick Kitson, public information officer for the Santa Clara County Department of Corrections, said the class-action against the jail system is currently being reviewed for summary judgement and that a judge has ordered the defendants not to comment on the case. "I couldn't comment on the specifics, but I can say that in fact the county is vigorously contesting the charges and for those individuals where there have been sustained findings and accusations, the Department of Corrections has vigorously pursued the full force and measure of the law to prosecute."

It's not just guards. Allegations of sexual abuse and harassment have been filed against prison ministers, doctors and male nurses, low-level administrators and even wardens. Sexual degradation and humiliation of women by staff is so ingrained in the culture of many women's prisons that it seems to have become an accepted mode of control in the custodial environment. In Washington, D.C., for example, quid pro quo sex with inmates was such a recognized part of the job for 20 or 30 years, says Brenda V. Smith, senior counsel of the National Women's Law Center, that it was considered an "attractive feature of the work environment."

The assumption: Once a woman enters a federal or state facility, she gives up all her rights, not only to her freedom and daily tasks, but to her body and to ward off sexual advances. Complicating the problem, of course, is that many women in prison have just left the streets, where the same thing was expected of them, whether they were prostitutes or addicts who gave up their bodies in return for drugs. At the same time, a huge proportion of women serving time have already been sexually victimized in their lives. According to Human Rights Watch, anywhere from 40 to 88 percent of incarcerated women have been victims of domestic violence and sexual or physical abuse either as children or adults. They have already been "conditioned" to believe that they deserve such treatment, and to remain silent, and the prison system plays on that vulnerability to intimidate them and keep them in line.

With those subjugative factors in place, it takes an extreme situation and an uncommonly strong and self-confident woman, like Lucas or Cruz, to tear down the wall of silence. "There's no reason to believe this was an isolated incident," said Lucas' lawyer, Geri Lynn Green, of her client's assault. "What was isolated about it was that someone came forward."

If anything, the problem is only becoming worse as the ranks of incarcerated women swell at an alarming rate. Today, the rate of increase of the female prison population has far outstripped the rate of men entering the system, and since 1980, the number of women in prison has risen by 400 percent. To keep up with the expanding population, the system needs more prisons. Since just 1990, the United States has built 16 new women's prisons, requiring the accelerated training and hiring of thousands of new guards. Not only has this made it more difficult for corrections departments to adequately train new recruits, says Brown, but it has disrupted the old, more civil, order of life in women's facilities. "When younger guards get out of line, it used to be there were older guards who would tell them not to do that," she says. "When you have prisons that are staffed by all new guards, there's no culture in place that says that no, it's not OK to do this with the women."

Jenni Gainsborough, public policy director for the National Prison Project of the American Civil Liberties Union, argues that the proportion of incidents of sexual misconduct may not be increasing at all, but that there are just more women who are talking. "One of the reasons we're hearing about it now is that there are more women in prisons, more male guards guarding them and more prisons," she says.

Too little, too late

When asked to respond to allegations of sexual misconduct by prison staff under its control, the U.S. Department of Justice says it "takes very seriously all allegations" of sexual misconduct. "Every allegation is reviewed and, where warranted, referred for criminal prosecution." Considering the large number of allegations, the number of actual prosecutions hasn't been overwhelming. According to the Justice Department's own records, only 10 prison employees in the entire federal system were disciplined in 1997 for sexual misconduct, and just seven were criminally prosecuted.

In March of 1998, the Federal Bureau of Prisons reached a settlement agreement with Robin Lucas and the other two Dublin inmates, agreeing not to house any more female inmates in the men's detention center, to create a confidential mechanism for reporting sexual assaults and to hire a consultant to review the prison's staff training programs. They also awarded the three women $500,000 to split. But the system has still not taken any of its employees to task for admitting male inmates into the cells of female inmates at night—for a fee.

The Justice Department claimed that an extensive investigation by its inspector general's office "did not establish sufficient evidence to prove under the standards for prosecution that any specific individual violated federal criminal law," and the U.S. Attorney's office in San Francisco and the Civil Rights Division in Washington, D.C., agreed.

No grounds for prosecution? Have they looked at Robin Lucas' face, to see the thick scar near her hairline where her head was smashed against her bunk, and the smaller scars on her arms and torso? Did they listen when she told them about how she still bleeds from her rectum? Perhaps they are conveniently hiding behind the fact that they never sent a doctor in to examine Lucas after the rape, never took blood samples from her cell and never collected any evidence on her behalf. Still, one has to wonder how a case that is worth $500,000 to the Federal Bureau of Prisons warrants no criminal charges against the assailants involved.

It's those kinds of questions that wrack Lucas' brain when she thinks about her share of the money.

"Is that what I had to go through?" she says. "Is that my compensation?" She has used some of the funds to renovate the board and care home and to buy certain amenities, like the new lawn mower. In May, she also used some to help her pay for a trip to Phoenix, where she tried out for the WNBA.

I follow Lucas through the narrow corridors of the basement and out to the small backyard where she shoots a couple of hoops and talks about the Justice Department's response to her claim. "These guys take an oath to protect and keep order," she says, missing her shot. "He broke that oath. But they're saying he didn't do anything wrong. That just fucks me up." She misses another shot, walks back toward the now-assembled mower and jerks its c ord, eliciting a violent roar.

"If I would have known that would have happened to me I would have ran," she shouts over the rumbling of the motor. "I would have ran to the ends of the earth."

Organizations to Contact

The editors have compiled the following list of organizations concerned with the issues debated in this book. The descriptions are derived from materials provided by the organizations. All have publications or information available for interested readers. The list was compiled on the date of publication of the present volume; the information provided here may change. Be aware that many organizations take several weeks or longer to respond to inquiries, so allow as much time as possible.

American Civil Liberties Union (ACLU) National Prison Project
1875 Connecticut Ave. NW, Suite 410, Washington, DC 20009
(202) 234-4830 • fax: (202) 234-4890
e-mail: aclu@aclu.org • website: http://www.aclu.org

Formed in 1972, the project serves as a national resource center and litigates cases to strengthen and protect adult and juvenile offenders' Eighth Amendment rights. It opposes electronic monitoring of offenders and the privatization of prisons. The project publishes the quarterly *National Prison Project Journal* and various booklets.

American Correctional Association (ACA)
4380 Forbes Blvd., Lanham, MD 20706-4322
(800) 222-5646 • (301) 918-1800 • fax: (301) 918-1900
e-mail: harryw@aca.org • website: http://www.corrections.com/aca

ACA is committed to improving national and international correctional policy and to promoting the professional development of those working in the field of corrections. It offers a variety of books and correspondence courses on corrections and criminal justice and publishes the bimonthly magazine *Corrections Today*.

Amnesty International (AI)
322 Eighth Ave., New York, NY 10001
(212) 807-8400 • fax: (212) 627-1451
website: http://www.amnesty-usa.org

Amnesty International is an independent worldwide movement working impartially for the release of all prisoners of conscience, fair and prompt trials for political prisoners, and an end to torture and executions. AI is funded by donations from its members and supporters throughout the world. The organization publishes books, reports, and the bimonthly *Amnesty International Newsletter*.

Campaign for an Effective Crime Policy
918 F St. NW, Suite 505, Washington, DC 20004
(202) 628-1903 • fax: (202) 628-1091
e-mail: info@crimepolicy.com • website: http://www.sproject.com/cecp.htm

Launched in 1992 by a group of criminal justice leaders, the nonpartisan Campaign for an Effective Crime Policy advocates alternative sentencing policies. It also works to educate the public about the relative effectiveness of various strategies for improving public safety. The campaign has published a series of reports on issues in criminal justice, including "'Three Strikes' Laws: Five Years Later."

Cato Institute
1000 Massachusetts Ave. NW, Washington, DC 20001-5403
(202) 842-0200 • fax: (202) 842-3490
e-mail: cato@cato.org • website: http://www.cato.org

The institute is a libertarian public policy research foundation dedicated to limiting the role of government and protecting individual liberties. The institute evaluates government policies and offers reform proposals in its publication *Policy Analysis.* Topics include "Prison Blues: How America's Foolish Sentencing Policies Endanger Public Safety" and "Crime, Police, and Root Causes." In addition, the institute publishes the quarterly magazine *Regulation,* the bimonthly *Cato Policy Report,* and numerous books.

Center for Alternative Sentencing and Employment Services (CASES)
346 Broadway, 8th Floor, New York, NY 10013
(212) 732-0076 • fax: (212) 571-0292
e-mail: careym@cases.org • website: http://www.cases.org/education/cases

CASES seeks to end what it views as the overuse of incarceration as a response to crime. It operates two alternative-sentencing programs in New York City: the Court Employment Project, which provides intensive supervision and services for felony offenders, and the Community Service Sentencing Project, which works with repeat misdemeanor offenders. The center advocates in court for such offenders' admission into its programs. CASES publishes various program brochures.

Families Against Mandatory Minimums (FAMM)
1612 K St. NW, Suite 1400, Washington, DC 20006
(202) 822-6700 • fax: (202) 822-6704
e-mail: famm@famm.org • website: http://www.famm.org

FAMM is an educational organization that works to repeal mandatory minimum sentences. It provides legislators, the public, and the media with information on and analyses of minimum-sentencing laws. FAMM publishes the quarterly newsletter *FAMM-gram.*

The Heritage Foundation
214 Massachusetts Ave. NE, Washington, DC 20002
(202) 546-4400 • fax: (202) 546-8328
e-mail: pubs@heritage.org • http://www.heritage.org

The Heritage Foundation is a conservative public policy research institute. It is a proponent of limited government and advocates tougher sentencing and the construction of more prisons. The foundation publishes articles on a variety of public policy issues in its Backgrounder series and in its quarterly journal *Policy Review.*

John Howard Society (JHS)
771 Montreal St., Kingston, ON, K7K 3J6 CANADA
(613) 542-7547 • fax: (613) 542-6824
e-mail: national@johnhoward.ca • website: http://www.johnhoward.ca

The John Howard Society of Canada advocates reform in the criminal justice system and monitors governmental policy to ensure fair and compassionate treatment of prisoners. It views imprisonment as a last resort option. The organization provides education to the community, support services to at-risk youth, and rehabilitation programs to former inmates. Its publications include the booklet *Literacy and the Courts: Protecting the Right to Understand.*

National Center for Policy Analysis (NCPA)
655 15th St. NW, Suite 375, Washington, DC 20005
(202) 628-6671 • fax: (202) 628-6474
e-mail: ncpa@public-policy.org • website: http://www.ncpa.org

NCPA is a nonprofit public policy research institute. It advocates more stringent prison sentences, the abolishment of parole, and restitution for crimes. Publications include the policy reports "Why Expected Punishment Deters Crime," "Parolees Return to Crime," and "Restitution Works for Juveniles."

National Center on Institutions and Alternatives (NCIA)
635 Slaters Lane, Suite G-100, Alexandria, VA 22314
(703) 684-0373 • fax: (703) 684-6037
website: http://www.ncianet.org/ncia

NCIA is a criminal justice foundation that encourages community-based alternatives to prison that are more effective in providing education, training, and personal skills required for the rehabilitation of nonviolent offenders. The center advocates doubling "good conduct" credit for the early release of nonviolent first-time offenders in the federal system to make room for violent offenders. NCIA publishes books, reports, and the periodic newsletters *Criminal Defense Update* and *Jail Suicide/Mental Health Update*.

National Crime Prevention Council (NCPC)
1700 K St. NW, 2nd Floor, Washington, DC 20006-3817
(202) 261-4111 • fax: (202) 296-1356
e-mail: webmaster@ncpc.org • website: http://www.ncpc.org

The NCPC provides training and technical assistance to groups and individuals interested in crime prevention. It advocates job training and recreation programs as a means to reduce crime and violence. The council, which sponsors the Take a Bite Out of Crime campaign, publishes the newsletter *Catalyst*, which is published ten times a year.

Police Foundation (PF)
1201 Connecticut Ave. NW, Washington, DC 20036
(202) 833-1460 • fax: (202) 659-9149
e-mail: pfinfo@policefoundation.org • website: http://www.policefoundation.org

The Police Foundation is committed to increasing police effectiveness in controlling crime, maintaining order, and providing humane and efficient service. The foundation sponsors forums that debate and disseminate ideas to improve personnel and practice in American criminal policing. It publishes a number of books, reports, and handbooks regarding all aspects of the criminal justice system.

Prison Fellowship Ministries (PFM)
PO Box 17500, Washington, DC 20041-0500
(703) 478-0100
website: http://www.prisonfellowship.org

Prison Fellowship Ministries encourages Christians to work in prisons and to assist communities in ministering to prisoners, ex-offenders, and their families. It works toward establishing a fair and effective criminal justice system and trains volunteers for in-prison ministries. Publications include the monthly *Jubilee* newsletter, the quarterly *Justice Report*, and numerous books, including *Born Again* and *Life Sentence*.

The Sentencing Project
918 F St. NW, Suite 501, Washington, DC 20004
(202) 628-0871 • fax: (202) 628-1091
e-mail: staff@sentencingproject.org • website: http://www.sentencingproject.org

The project seeks to provide public defenders and other public officials with information on establishing and improving alternative sentencing programs that provide convicted persons with positive and constructive options to incarceration. It promotes increased public understanding of the sentencing process and alternative sentencing programs. It publishes the reports "Americans Behind Bars: A Comparison of International Rates of Incarceration" and "Young Black Men and the Criminal Justice System: A Growing National Problem."

U.S. Department of Justice
Federal Bureau of Prisons
320 First St. NW, Washington, DC 20534
e-mail: webmaster@bop.gov • website: http://www.bop.gov

The Federal Bureau of Prisons works to protect society by confining offenders in the controlled environments of prison and community-based facilities. It believes in providing work and other self-improvement opportunities within these facilities to assist offenders in becoming law-abiding citizens. The bureau publishes the book *The State of the Bureau*.

Bibliography

Books

Gary Cornelius	*Jails in America: An Overview of Issues*. 2nd ed. Lanham, MD: American Correctional Association, 1996.
Michael Jacobson Hardy	*Behind the Razor Wire: Portrait of a Contemporary American Prison System*. New York: New York University Press, 1998.
Nancy R. Jacobs, Jacquelyn F. Quiran, and Mark A. Siegel, eds.	*Crime: A Serious American Problem*. Wylie, TX: Information Plus, 1996.
Kenneth E. Kerle	*American Jails: Looking to the Future*. Woburn, MA: Butterworth-Heinemann, 1998.
Ken Lamberton	*Wilderness and Razor Wire*. San Francisco: Mercury House, 1999.
Marilyn D. McShane and Frank P. Williams, eds.	*Encyclopedia of American Prisons*. New York: Garland, 1996.
Marilyn Tower Oliver	*Prisons: Today's Debate*. Springfield, NJ: Enslow, 1997.
Edward E. Rhine, ed.	*Best Practices: Excellence in Corrections*. Lanham, MD: American Correctional Association, 1998.
Clive Sharp	*How to Survive Federal Prison Camp: A Guidebook for Those Caught Up in the System*. Port Townsend, WA: Loompanics Unlimited, 1997.
Kathryn Watterson	*Women in Prison: Inside the Concrete Womb*. Boston, MA: Northeastern University Press, 1996.
Michael Welch	*Corrections: A Critical Approach*. Columbus, OH: McGraw Hill College Division, 1996.

Periodicals

Sasha Abramsky and Andrew White	"Rage in the Cage," *City Limits*, June/July 1996. Available from 120 Wall St., 20th Floor, New York, NY 10005.
Amnesty International	"Rights for All," October 1998. Available from Amnesty International, 1 Easton St., London, England WC1X0DJ.
Jeff Anderson	"A Prescription for Disaster?" *Prison Mirror*, December, 1997. Available from 970 Pickett St. North, Bayport, MN 55003-1490.
Anne-Marie Cusac	"Shock Value: U.S. Stun Devices Pose Human Rights Risk," *Progressive*, September 1997.

102

Nat Hentoff

"Our 'Overprivileged' Prisoners," *Washington Post*, March 29, 1997. Available from 1150 15th St. NW, Washington, DC 20071.

Debra Jo Immergut

"Disenfranchising the Powerless," *Tikkun*, May/June 1999. Available from P.O. Box 460926, Escondido, CA 92046.

Issues and Controversies On File

"Prisoners' Rights," November 20, 1998. Available from Facts On File News Services, 11 Penn Plaza, New York, NY 10001-2006.

Jeff Jacoby

"The Puritan Approach to Dealing with Crime," *Conservative Chronicle*, March 5, 1997. Available from Box 29, Hampton, IA 50441.

Kevin Johnson

"New Prisons Isolate Worst Inmates," *USA Today*, August 4, 1997.

Peter Kilborn

"Revival of Chain Gangs Takes a Twist," *New York Times*, March 11, 1997.

Drew Leder

"It's Our Christian Duty to Educate Prisoners," *U.S. Catholic*, March 1996.

Marjorie Lemon

"Prison Libraries Change Lives," *Information Outlook*, November 1997. Available from 1700 E 18th St. NW, Washington, DC 20009-2514.

Kerry Myers

"Measuring Up," *Angolite*, January/February 1997. Available from Louisiana State Penitentiary, Angola, LA 70712.

Roger T. Pray

"How Did Our Prisons Get This Way?" *Prison Mirror*, May 1996.

William Raspberry

"America—the World's Busiest Jailer," *Washington Post*, December 14, 1999.

Andrew A. Skolnick

"Critics Denounce Staffing Jails and Prisons with Physicians Convicted of Misconduct," *Journal of the American Medical Association*, October 28, 1998. Available from 515 N. State St., Chicago, IL 60610.

Jon Marc Taylor

"The Great Dumbbell Theft," *Prison News Service*, Spring 1996. Available from PSC Publishers, Box 5052, Station A, Toronto, ON MSW 1W4 Canada.

Index

advance directives, 72, 77–78
AFL-CIO, 31
African Americans
  impact of disenfranchisement
    laws, 40
  incarceration rates for, 45–46
AIDS/HIV
  cost of care for, 74
  prevalence in prison
    population, 73–74
"All Too Familiar: Sexual
  Abuse of Women in U.S.
  State Prisons" (Human
  Rights Watch), 93
American Civil Liberties
  Union (ACLU), 60
American Correctional
  Association, 69
Americans with Disabilities
  Act, 78
Amnesty International, 7
Armstrong, John J., 36
Arpaio, Joe, 8, 37
Auburn system, 53, 54

Badger State Industries, 29
Bailey, Emmanuel H., 24
Barry, Ellen, 92
Body Orifice Scanning System
  (BOSS), 24
Boston, John, 25
British Forensic Science
  Service, 66
Brunstorf, Kowwani, 25
Bureau of Justice Statistics
  on disenfranchisement of

inmates, 45
Burger, Warren E., 28
Butler, Kevin, 22

California Department of
  Corrections, 16
chain gangs
  costs of, 86–87
  education and training are
    better options, 87–88
  history of, 86
  should be abolished, 85–88
Chamber of Commerce, U.S.,
  31
Chasan, Jonathan S., 21, 25
Civil Rights of
  Institutionalized Persons Act,
  33
Colorado State Penitentiary,
  53
Commissioner of Corrections v.
  Myers, 75
compassionate release, 76, 79
  costs of, 80
Conyers, John, Jr., 47
Cover, John H., 63, 66
Cruz, Elly, 94–95
Cruz v. Vasquez, 95
Cybulski Correctional
  Institution, 34

Dellelo, Robert, 52
disenfranchisement laws
  history of, 41
  implementing change in, 49
  numbers affected by, 43

and incarceration policies,
44–45
in other countries, 48
racial impact of, 41, 43–44
restoration of vote under, 42
states enforcing, 40
disparity among, 42
states' interest in, 47
Douthit, Raquel, 92
Doyle, Christine M., 25
Drew, Christopher, 20
drug offenses
and black incarceration rates,
46
Dubler, Nancy Neveloff, 71

elderly
in prison population, 74
end-of-life care
goals of, 81
humane, inmates should
receive, 71–81
litigation over, 80–81
Estelle v. Gamble, 80

Federal Prison Industries, 32
Fellner, Jamie, 40
Filiaggi, James, 69
Flanagan, Timothy, 35, 38

Gainsborough, Jenni, 38, 60,
96
gangs
and prison violence, 22
Gaston, George, 36
Gill, Howard, 28
Giuliani, Rudolph, 20, 22
Gramm, Phil, 28
Grassian, Stuart, 52, 56, 60
Graves, George, 11
Green, Geri Lynn, 96
Gyatso, Palden, 67

Haney, Craig, 55, 56
Harrington, Spencer P.M., 51
health care, 7
for HIV-infected inmates,
cost of, 74
at Pelican Bay State Prison, 18
in prisons and jails, 75
Hill, James, 25
HIV. *See* AIDS/HIV
Hoffman, Phil, 6
Horan, John R., 26
Houston Chronicle (newspaper),
33
Human Rights Watch, 40, 93

incarceration
history of, 6
rate of, in U.S., 6
effects of sentencing policies
on, 44–45
inmates
and guards
laws against sexual activity
between, 94
mentally ill, in supermax
prisons, 52, 58–60
numbers of
over age 55, 74
HIV-infected, 73–74
privileges as management
tool, 37
recreation/educational
programs for make sense,
34–39
should receive humane end-
of-life care, 71–81
stun devices should not be
used to control, 62–70
International Covenant on Civil
and Political Rights, 68

Jacobson, Michael P., 22, 23
Jemelka, Ron, 59

Justice Department, U.S.
  sexual harassment lawsuits of,
    92
  on sexual misconduct by
    prison guards, 97

Kaufman, Dennis, 64
Keaton, Willie Kelly, Jr., 35
Kerik, Bernard, 20, 23, 26
King, Rodney, 63
Kissel, John A., 36
Kitson, Rick, 95
Kronzer, Steve, 29

LaBelle, Debra, 94
labor, prison, 7
  benefits to
    the economy, 27–33
    prisoners from, 29
  public policy reforms needed,
    32–33
  restrictions on, 29–30
  taxpayer savings from, 28–29
Limbaugh, Rush, 14
living wills, 72
Lovell, David, 58, 59
Lucas, Robin, 89–91, 96, 97

Madrid v. Gomez, 53, 55
Maricopa County jail system,
  8–10, 37–38
  food service, 10–13
Marshall, Thurgood
  on disenfranchisement laws,
    46–47
Maryland Correctional
  Adjustment Center, 53
Mauer, Marc, 40
Maynard, Sean, 26
McGreevy, Tim, 66
Meares, Tracy L., 85
medical care. *See* health care

Mercadel, Valerie, 92
Milgram, Stanley, 65, 70
Murcelo, William, 39

National Advisory
  Commission on Criminal
  Justice Standards and Goals,
  47
National Rifle Association, 63
New York Post (newspaper),
  12–13

Office of U.S. Pardon
  Attorney, 42, 43
officers, correctional
  male, in women's facilities,
    93–94
  value recreational/educational
    amenities, 34–35
  survey on, 38

Pelican Bay State Prison, 53,
  55
  Security Housing Unit
    accommodation of legal
      research, 18–19
    design of, 17
    eligibility for, 16–17
    inmate restrictions in,
      17–18
    use of inmate leisure time, 19
Penal Reform International, 48
penitentiaries
  history of, 53–55
Pennsylvania system, 53, 54
pepper spray, 22, 23
Post Release Employment
  Project, 29
Prison Litigation Reform Act, 60
prisons
  recreational/educational
    amenities in

provide incentives for good behavior, 38–39
should be uncomfortable for prisoners, 8–15
U.S., population of, 27, 71
mentally ill among, 59
women among, 91

recreation, for inmates
criticism of, 36
is beneficial, 35–36
rehabilitation
is incompatible with prisons, 53
and Pennsylvania system, 54
Reynolds, Morgan O., 27
Rheinstein, John, 55
Richardson v. Ramirez, 47
Rideau, Larry, 71
Rights for All (Amnesty International), 7
Rikers Island prison, 20–26
Robinson, Charles, 34
Rowland, John G., 36
Russo, Frank, 10

Sam Houston State University, 38
Sawicki, Sandra, 35
Schulz, William F., 62
Schumpeter, Joseph, 31
Sealy, Deshawn, 25
sentencing policies
effects on incarceration rates, 45
Sentencing Project
survey on impact of disenfranchisement laws, 41
sexual abuse
criminalization of, 94
of female inmates, is widespread, 89–97
Siegal, Nina, 89

Silverstein, Thomas, 54
Smith, Brenda V., 93, 96
solitary confinement
psychological effects of, 57
Start, Armand, 66
Stratbucker, Robert A., 66
stun devices, 21
danger of misuse abroad, 67–68
health risks of, 65–67
should not be used to control prisoners, 62–70
states prohibiting, 63
use as torture devices, 25
Stun Tech, 63–64
Suedfeld, Peter, 57, 58
Sumner-Ashurst Act, 32
supermax prisons, 6
are cruel and inhumane, 51–61
attempts at reform of, 52–53
modern history of, 54–55
psychological effects of confinement in, 55–58
violent offender should be placed in, 16–19
Supreme Court
interpretation of cruel and unusual punishment, 60
surveys
of correctional officials on amenities, 38

Taser device, 63
Thomas, Andrew Peyton, 30
Thompson, Tommy, 28
three-strikes laws, 44
Tofig, Dana, 34
torture
use of stun devices in, 67–68
Toughest Sheriff in America, The (Arpaio), 37

Vacco v. Quill, 80
Valdez, Edward, 62
Vanoudenhove, Scott, 38
Verdeyen, Robert, 52
violence, in prison
  strict discipline lowers,
    20–26
voting rights. *See*
  disenfranchisement laws

Walker Special Management
  Unit, 35

Walsh-Healy Act, 32
Washington v. Glucksberg, 80
Wilson, Amanda, 94
women
  incarceration rates of, 45
  numbers of, incarcerated, 91
  sexual abuse of, is widespread,
    89–97

Yates, Joseph C., 89

Zonana, Howard, 59